The Socio-Economic Transformation

The Socio-Economic Transformation

Getting Closer to What?

Edited by

Zbigniew Nahorski

Jan W. Owsiński

Tomasz Szapiro

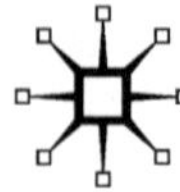

First published 2007 by
PALGRAVE MACMILLAN
Houndmills, Basingstoke, Hampshire RG21 6XS and
175 Fifth Avenue, New York, N.Y. 10010
Companies and representatives throughout the world

PALGRAVE MACMILLAN is the global academic imprint of the Palgrave Macmillan division of St. Martin's Press, LLC and of Palgrave Macmillan Ltd. Macmillan® is a registered trademark in the United States, United Kingdom and other countries. Palgrave is a registered trademark in the European Union and other countries.

ISBN 13: 978–0–230–00794–9 hardback
ISBN 10: 0–230–00794–5 hardback

This book is printed on paper suitable for recycling and made from fully managed and sustained forest sources.

A catalogue record for this book is available from the British Library.

Library of Congress Cataloging-in-Publication Data

The Socio-economic transformation : getting closer to what? / edited by Zbigniew Nahorski, Jan W. Owsiński, Tomasz Szapiro.
p. cm.
Includes bibliographical references and index.
Contents: Pt. I. Institutional transformation: the ownership paradigm – pt. 2. Redistribution, government, technology, and human capital.
ISBN 13: 978–0–230–00794–9 (cloth)
ISBN 10: 0–230–00794–5 (cloth)
1. Europe, Eastern–Economic policy–1989– 2. Former Soviet republics–Economic policy. 3. Social change–Europe, Eastern. 4. Social change–Former Soviet republics. I. Nahorski, Zbigniew, 1945– II. Owsiński, J. W. (Jan W.). III. Szapiro, Tomasz.

HC244.S5913 2007
338.947–dc22 2006049070

10 9 8 7 6 5 4 3 2 1
16 15 14 13 12 11 10 09 08 07

Printed and bound in Great Britain by
Antony Rowe Ltd, Chippenham and Eastbourne

Contents

List of Tables and Figures

Tables

Figures

Preface

The present volume resulted from a rather lengthy process of writing, reviewing, and editing, in which quite a number of persons and institutions have been involved. The starting point was constituted by an international conference held in Warsaw, devoted to the broad subject of transition to the advanced market institutions and economies. It was decided at that meeting that the themes discussed may be of real interest to several audiences, and that it would be good to work on three different volumes, with contents based upon the directions of these discussions. Thus, three different book-writing processes were set in motion. The first of the books appeared as the issue of the *Annals of Operations Research* at the very end of 2000, edited by the same team as the present one. In accordance with the profile of the series, the book contained papers devoted to the technical aspects of transition in the domains of political institutions (e.g. voting procedures), managerial approaches, financial markets, and so on. The second book was published in 2001 by the University of Information Technology and Management in Warsaw. It focussed on the econometric modelling and analysis of the economies in transition. The present volume was meant to provide a broader perspective on the actual and potential systemic changes and their directions. Hence, the majority of studies contained here are devoted to exploration of the space of possible fundamental solutions for the countries in transition, involving both their economic and political systems.

All the papers went through a careful refereeing procedure, a broad team of scholars from around the world participated. In terms of institutions having contributed to the emergence of this, and, indeed, the two other, books, the network involved was composed of the Systems Research Institute of the Polish Academy of Sciences, the Polish Operational and Systems Research Society, the International Federation of the Operational Research Societies (IFORS), as well as the EURO Working Group MODEST, affiliated with the IFORS' European chapter, EURO.

It is obvious for any observer of today's world that the accelerated pace of changes, which started in the late 1980s, has not much slowed down and that a vast proportion of the economic-and-political systems of the world are still involved in an active search for the optimum paths. We hope that the studies presented here will constitute source of inspiration for those who try to think of the future in a bold, and at the same time organised manner, and for those who may have an influence upon it.

THE EDITORS

Notes on the Contributors

Authors of papers
in the order of appearance of papers in the book

Leonid Hurwicz is among the greatest of the living economists. His contribution to the economic theory and to a number of its quantitative aspects has a fundamental character. To name a few domains of his essential contribution: stability of competitive equilibria, decision theory, allocation mechanisms, as well as economic and institutional design. In 1990 Leonid Hurwicz was awarded with the National Medal of the President of the United States, since 1965 he has been a member of the American Academy of Arts and Sciences, and he became a member of the US National Academy of Sciences in 1974. He is Doctor *Honoris Causa* of several universities, including the University of Chicago, Northwestern, Keyo (Tokyo), Barcelona, and Warsaw School of Economics.

Philipp J.H. Schröder is Associate Professor in Economics at the Aarhus School of Business in Denmark. He has been before a Senior Economist at the German Institute for Economic Research and has worked in management consulting. His research interests are within international economics, transition economics, the economics of Open Source Software, and issues surrounding European integration.

Thorvaldur Gylfason is Professor of Economics at the University of Iceland, Editor of the *European Economic Review*, and Research Fellow at CEPR (Centre for Economic Policy Research) in London, as well as at CESifo (Center for Economic Studies) at the University of Munich. He has published over 100 scholarly articles and fifteen books, including seven collections of essays in Icelandic, and *Understanding the Market Economy* (1992), which has appeared in 17 languages, as well as *Principles of Economic Growth* (1999). He writes a weekly column for Iceland's largest daily newspaper, *Fréttablaðið*.

Jan W. Owsiński is an adjoint professor at the Systems Research Institute of the Polish Academy of Sciences in Warsaw, heading the Department of Systems Methods Applications. Author of more than 150 papers and editor of some 25 volumes, of which majority in English. Together with Zbigniew Nahorski manages the Working Group MODEST of EURO. Main scientific interests include data analysis with applications in economics (especially international trade), market analysis, modeling of transition processes, and decision support.

Jean-Luc Schneider is Deputy Assistant Secretary, in charge of the Macroeconomic Analysis Department at the French Treasury. He has been working as economist and consultant for the Fiscal Affairs Department of the International Monetary Fund for the past 15 years. Jean-Luc Schneider is also Vice-chairman of the WP1 of OECD's Economic Policy Committee.

Scott Baier is an Assistant Professor of Economics at Clemson University. He is also a visiting scholar at the Federal Reserve Bank of Atlanta. His areas of interest include international trade, economic growth, and economic development. He has also served on the faculty at the University of Notre Dame.

Gerhard Glomm is a Professor of Economics at Indiana University in Bloomington. His main interests are in macroeconomics and public finance. He devoted an important part of his research to education finance. He is also a member of the CESifo network.

Milan Zeleny is the most cited of all Czech economists. He is a Professor of Management Systems at Fordham University, and Visiting Professor at the Xidian University in Xi'an, China and at the Tomas Bata University in Zlín, Czech Republic. He is the author of some 400 papers, editor-in-chief of *Human Systems Management.* His most recent books include *Human Systems Management*, *Information Technology in Business* (Thomson) and *New Frontiers of Decision Making for the Information Technology Era.*

Mikhail Mikhalevich graduated from Kiev State University in 1978 with speciality Economic Cybernetics. Now he is a chair of the department of systems analysis at the Ukrainian Academy of Foreign Trade and lectures at such Ukrainian universities as the Kyiv Mohyla Academy and National Shevchenko University. He is a Member of the National Academy of Sciences of Ukraine. The area of his scientific interests includes: modelling of the transition economy (macroeconomic models, analysis of inflation, and theory of cycles), decision theory (preference optimization problems, utility theory for non-transitive preferences), multicriteria analysis and numerical methods of optimization. Mikhail Mikhalevich published more than 140 scholarly articles and five books. He was awarded the Glushkov (1995) and Ostrovsky (1982) prizes.

Zbigniew Nahorski is a Professor at the Systems Research Institute, Polish Academy of Sciences, where he heads the Laboratory of Computer Modelling. He is also the Dean of the Computer Science Department, Warsaw School of Information Technology. Zbigniew Nahorski is the Editor-in-Chief of the journal *Control and Cybernetics*. Together with Jan W. Owsiński manages the Working Group MODEST of EURO. He is the author of over 150 scholarly papers and four books, as well as the editor of 25 books or special issues of technical journals. His research interests are related to the modelling of environmental, economic and medical systems, including environmental economic models. His areas of interest also include methods and algorithms of statistical model building, optimization and control, and data analysis, particularly for dynamic systems.

Tomasz Szapiro is a Professor at the Warsaw School of Economics (WSE), the Head of Division of Decision Analysis and Support in the Institute of Econometrics at WSE. Former Dean of the WSE Graduate School. He is also Professor at the Institute for Modern Civilization of WSE, Adjunct Professor of International Business Studies at Carlson School of Business, University of Minneapolis, Minnesota, and a member of the American-Polish Executive MBA Council. Published more than 120 papers, two books and a monograph. Worked as expert for the Ministries of Finance and of Education, as well as for UNIDO, European Commission, and Fulbright Commission. His research interests are in mathematical modeling of economic processes, theory, analysis and support for decision making, and economics of education.

Some Remarks on the Study of Transformation Processes: the Wisdom in and the Limitations of Models

Zbigniew Nahorski, Jan W. Owsiński and Tomasz Szapiro

1

The world's economic systems are going currently through a number of transformation processes of more or less dramatic nature. These particular processes, which have been taking place in the post-socialist part of the globe are perhaps the most vivid among all those that change the world's economy and its societies. Certainly, the definitely fundamental character of changes entailed by the post-socialist transition provides a motivation for returning to the study of many of the issues which have already some time ago dropped from the agenda of mainstream of economic thought, or to study some other essential issues against the light of new evidence. (This applies in a particular manner to the question of the limits to state intervention in the economic systems.) Thus, it would be indeed incorrect to think of analyses of the transitory processes as uniquely or even primarily oriented at these economies in which the truly dramatic changes have been or still are taking place. The actual implications of such studies ought to be valid for all of the economic and social systems of the globe.

During the so deep transformations the mechanisms governing the socioeconomic processes get most radically uncovered, the secondary effects subsiding to the background. So, the significance of the actual transformation processes also lies in the fact that they provide empirical evidence to feed the more general propositions and methods, which belong either to the theoretical or to policy domains. Yet, together with such possibility, resulting from the occurrence of the transition processes, there goes the very high level of uncertainty in the records of these processes. This provides an additional breeding ground for various interpretations of the existing or new propositions, oftentimes of clearly ideological origin.

Thus, whatever theoretical construct or policy-oriented suggestion is being validated against the course of the transition processes, utmost care must be taken to make sure the validation procedure is properly performed, that under the apparent surface of things the actual reality, and not a political image of it, is being considered. The now available toolbox of formal data analysis allows for an effective performance of such validation endeavours, without which one is often confronted with noise rather than a clear message.

The transition economies offer a testbed. They are a testbed for concepts and theories, for broader ideas and for the methods of scientific inquiry, but also for the multiplicity of ideological interpretations. Designing the strategies for the transition processes and testing the theories relative to economic, social and political change constitute an unprecedented challenge to intellectual capacity of the scientific community.

2

If we concentrate on the processes taking place in the post-socialist part of the world, then we can see an extremely wide variety of situations and of patterns of evolution over time. It can be rightly suspected that application of the same sort of policies to different initial socio-economic conditions of a country will bring completely different effects. This may be regarded as a case known from the theory of sensitivity of differential equations, where a very small (even infinitely small) change of parameters may lead to entirely different system behaviour. While providing a good metaphor, such theories, if treated seriously, have to refer, though, to quite precise formulations in terms of both descriptions of mechanisms and of the concrete parameter values. As long as these parameters are not well known a lot is left to interpretation, as indicated before. That is why the point of view of the analyst may define so much in the presented image of transformation.

An excellent illustration for the opportunity ('testbed') of observing unique courses of events and true-to-life testing of some theories is provided by the radical policy and legal moves made in some of the post-communist European countries. Take linear taxation, introduced first in Estonia, and then considered seriously in some other countries, or drastic lowering of taxes in Slovakia, and the (positive) effects thereof. Indeed, it may be argued that these are economies - and societies - of a somewhat special character. Such a sweeping statement is, however, in no way an equivalent of explanation.

Indeed it is so that the starting point, the society and the economy subject to transformation, determines to a large extent the course of processes which are meant to be guided by certain explicit policies. One must look, therefore, at the 'robust' characteristics of such starting points and the equally 'robust' theories, which can be genuinely, applied to the deep transformation processes, showing their fundamental features and the basic choices available. While being adequately robust vis à vis the epiphenomena, as distinct from the true deeper characteristics, such theories and methods thereof must also be appropriately 'fine' so as to discern among the various courses of events and among the manners in which respective (for instance, institutional) solutions and policy instruments are to be applied.

3

The present volume contains a selection of studies devoted to the essential issues of transformation, residing, at the same time, in the key points of the economic theory. They include the issues from institutional design, the property right settings, the share and the role of the government, the redistribution paradigm, the role of human capital, the macroeconomic decisions to be made, etc. Unavoidably, the studies here contained highlight the particular issues from a definite perspective, even if providing quite general thought frameworks. In the opinion of the present editors it is these frameworks that are here of utmost importance. Although many of the conclusions forwarded seem to be deeply justified, some other call for additional analysis, in order to, in particular, get rid of a bias weighing on them. Thus, the frameworks proposed constitute a set of instruments for further analysing and then designing the transformation processes.

4

The volume starts with the study by **Leonid Hurwicz** on the possibility of modelling institutional settings and their changes in the language of and with the methods developed in game theory. Indeed, institutional change is in the heart of the transformation, especially the post-socialist one. The importance of effort devoted to modelling and design of institutions cannot be overestimated. The analysis offered by Hurwicz in this volume is just an introduction into the domain, providing initial definitions and some of their implications and interpretations. Hurwicz calls, in particular, for a finer distinction than just 'market' and 'plan' to distinguish the institutional paradigms. This, indeed, is a proper intellectual challenge in the world fraught with imperfect or mixed institutional settings, which, in addition, evolve in time. Yet, not only is modelling of such intermediate settings difficult (since they cannot usually be simply expressed by a parameter value ranging between 0 and 1, like in the example shown by Hurwicz), but the setting is, as a rule, much more complex, involving power interrelations. Hurwicz argues, however, that the game-theoretic framework allows for avoiding the looming infinite regression trap. In particular, it has been the experience of many a socialist society that gradual or step-wise abandonment of the socialist regime was not possible because only complete dismantling of the entire existing power structure could be a warrant for the actual possibility of any substantial change. Otherwise, this structure would always act in the direction of preservation of the *status quo ante*. This volume contains yet some other analyses, which also refer to similar problems, especially those by Philipp Schröder and Jan W. Owsiński in the first part of the book, and by Jean-Luc Schneider, which opens the second part of it. These other studies highlight some of the specific aspects of modelling, analysis, as well as dynamics of various paradigms referring to institutional setting and ownership.

A very interesting study by **Philipp J.H. Schröder** takes up a problem tightly associated with the preceding one: namely the potential shareholder-stakeholder conflict, which may be of paramount importance in the context of mass privatisation processes, taking place in the post-communist economies and societies. The analysis is indeed of high significance given that privatisation has led to a variety of social and economic effects, in particular - in terms of productivity. This variety is apparent both across the different economies and within them. The model, proposed by Schröder, makes it possible to analyse various configurations of respective parameters, and find the ones, for which the shareholder-stakeholder conflict is not a problem. It is highly interesting to note that some of the aspects touched upon in the paper (e.g. the positive stake in the inefficiency of a firm) are very closely related to what Owsiński takes up later on in the book.

The next paper in the first part of the book presents the study by **Thorvaldur Gylfason**, who makes certain assumptions in his model of growth which give rise to a discussion with the considerations of Schröder's. Thus, although it is beyond dispute that privatisation ought to lead to improved efficiency, this is not always the case, and, moreover, the actual parameters are hard to grasp, unless a separate study is undertaken (anyway, very much worth the money potentially put into it). The elegant model proposed by Gylfason offers, however, a very good starting point for elaboration of a broader (where can we stop generalising?) model structure, in which efficiency gains would be appropriately endogenised. In view of the still continuing search for the growth-securing institutional settings (and not only just the 'parameters', like tax systems and levels), a growth model that takes into consideration the institutional changes, like the one proposed by Gylfason, is certainly of very high value.

The first part of the book ends with the paper by **Jan W. Owsiński**, presenting the so-called 'herring barrel metaphor' and its consequences. The verbal metaphor, a simple, but powerful image of the way the communist system worked, is in fact a quasi-model, without numbers, which shows most of the essential aspects of the system. In particular, it shows that shortage was not just an aspect, even if very important, or unavoidable, of the system. It proves that shortage was indeed the core of the system, and its basis. Shortage was the source of exchange power, and led to the setting, in which money was of secondary importance, labour productivity naturally declined, and labour shortage appeared. The paper shows also how the system had to collapse, sooner or later, under its weight, but, perhaps, with quite a variety of different consequences. This variety includes, as an essential issue, the one already discussed in the book, namely: the way, in which privatisation is performed.

At this point, with the issue of privatisation (and re-privatisation, still a point of public debate in Poland) and growth, we have reached the stage of consideration of the theoretical and political dilemma of efficiency *versus* (or better: *and*) redistribution. Either in the form of explicit policies or of the deeper institutional settings, the question of normative vs. positive returns on almost every path of reasoning, and has to be accounted for in the models elaborated.

Thus, we have already mentioned the model elaborated by **Jean-Luc Schneider**, which opens the second part of the book. This very appealing model, related in a way to the social choice theory, is meant to explain the apparently non-rational behaviour of voters choosing between the somewhat parabolic 'socialism' and 'capitalism'. Side by side with the convincing structure of the model, and a generally confirming 'oscillatory' behaviour of the electorates in the formerly socialist statehoods, there is also, by the way of this paper, a very interesting sociological study done in Poland yet at the beginning of the 1980s, which shows, among blue collar workers, a high degree of rejection of the communism and, at the same time, high level of reluctance to working in a privately owned company. Again, the conclusions from this model - and yet other than expected by the author - are largely corroborated by the experience of the socialist societies. This, in particular, applies to the gradual change option analysed in the framework of the model. In the perspective of a 'voter' the result implying approval of the gradual change is definitely correct, as distinct from the necessity of 'breaking away' mentioned before: the difference lies in the perspective (either a subjective perspective of a voter or an 'objective' view of a designer). The voters know very well the preferred direction of change, but for many reasons opt for small, gradual changes or may even choose the option inconsistent with their own essential preference. An especially interesting aspect of this paper is constituted by the stability issue, so important in the actual economic and political life.

Scott Baier and **Gerhard Glomm** look at the share taken by the state in the overall national economy, with a view on its influence on the growth rate, and reach perhaps a not-too-surprising, but rather well justified conclusion that even small decreases in the state's bite may have a significant positive impact on the growth rates of the economy as a whole. Likewise, disbursements from the state budget are more likely to enhance the growth rate when they are directed towards investments rather than consumption. Although such a conclusion could be treated as next to trivial and, by some, irrelevant, it is not without deeper significance, and this not only for the economies and societies in transition. Once the drive towards the more and more caring and powerful welfare state has been put to doubt, and reversed, and then this reversal, in turn, questioned, the problem posed - and analysed - by Baier and Glomm is in the focus of many a growth debate. The proposition that there are 'reasonable' policy levels in this respect is, of course, void as long as these are not determined for the particular economies and development stages. Since the present editors share the view conform to the results from the model, it is only with pleasure that we note both the structure of and the conclusions from it.

Milan Zeleny, who worked for a long time in optimization algorithms and their applications, takes a look at kind of transition that all the economies and societies appear to be confronted with: the challenge of information and knowledge. Zeleny argues that business education for the twenty first century ought to centre on 'wisdom', as transgressing the limits of not only just 'data', or 'information' derived from data, or even 'knowledge' that synthesises information. In the eyes of Zeleny, wisdom is the faculty associated with the question 'why?', and the capacity of answering it, not in the technological, but a broader perspective. In this context, wisdom tends to be intertwined with ethics and morality, as well as actual additional value, especially for the customer. It is argued that education, or expansion of the human and social capital, should take these crucial aspects into account, and that without them the undertakings such as the 'Lisbon strategy' will have to fail.

The book closes with the paper by **Mikhail Mikhalevich**, presenting a model of a labour market in a specific set of circumstances, which are particularly pertinent for the case of Ukraine. The model represents the monophonic labour market against the background of the market of goods and services. As is the case with other similar models, even a relatively simple structure, endowed with dynamics, displays quite complex behaviour, including, in particular, potential oscillations. These are of special significance for the understanding of the course of events in countries like Ukraine. But they may, as well, be of interest for a wider set of economies and societies, where the labour market, and, more generally, human capital, is subject to similar conditions. In this way the analysis of relations between the institutions and the human capital takes a full round.

5

Models may not constitute satisfactorily detailed reflections of the real world. Umberto Eco, however, pointed out already the impossibility of producing a one-to-one map of the empire, and so we are doomed to use only such projections of reality that we can readily handle. In fact, we always use models (speak prose, Molière), even if we do not know about this, though these are often just mental models, describing the reality and the mechanisms which govern it (if it is raining, the traffic jams will get worse). All intelligible concepts and theories are based upon, or are themselves, such models. Putting them on paper, formalising them, and making them public allows for a reasoned debate, in which the cerebral 'variables' are more easily separated from logical constructs and actual data. Although we are well aware that for many problems there may not exist the ultimate (optimal, rational) solutions (whether obtained owing to the explicit use of models or not), we believe that in all cases we might be able to make definite improvements for the good of all, if we know more. The thought frameworks presented and discussed in this book are meant to provide instruments just for this.

Part I

Institutional Transformation: The Ownership Paradigm

Chapter 1

An Essay in Modeling of Institutional Change

Leonid Hurwicz

Economic analysis carried out with the help of models has been suffering from a lack of expression of institutional settings. Yet institutional change is at the heart of numerous transition processes around the globe. This chapter illustrates a way of modelling ***institutional arrangements*** *through the game theoretic framework, involving utility functions and game-forms. Illustrative analysis is provided for a well-defined classical case of land tenure institutions. Then, the chapter gives an analysis of a broader domain involving law-making, its effectiveness and enforcement. The chapter implies that the limits to market mechanisms ought to be taken into account when designing the institutional frameworks for the transition societies and economies.*

1.1 Introduction

In recent decades institutional changes have been the central economic events across the globe. The dominant trend, both East and West, has been a movement toward decentralization and markets, and away from regulation, command, and central planning.

It is to be noted, however, that in the international sphere contrary phenomena are also observed. The formation of customs unions, the proposed currency unification in Western Europe, and the increased power of international lending agencies (the IMF, the World Bank), especially during periods of economic difficulties, shift some of the decision-making authority from countries to international bodies, thus introducing an element of centralization.

The present volume, devoted to these processes, is both timely and important.

Until recently the existing techniques employed in economic analysis were rather inadequate to provide guidance in analyzing institutional change and its consequences.

One reason for this was the lack of formal models explicitly incorporating economic institutional arrangements. While prevailing models presuppose specific institutional arrangements, with rare exceptions these arrangements are not displayed explicitly as ‘variables’ or ‘unknowns’ of the problem.

Secondly, there has been a tendency to concentrate on equilibrium states and on comparative statics rather than on the dynamics of transition. The emphasis of this volume on transition phenomena offers therefore a valuable contrast.

Thirdly, there has been a traditional focus on the idealized perfectly competitive ('Walrasian') economies, with little progress being made in the understanding of imperfectly competitive phenomena in a general (as opposed to partial) equilibrium setting. A consequence of this latter weakness has been a tendency to apply the perfectly competitive model to situations rich in monopoly and oligopoly elements - either 'natural' monopoly (due, for example, to the presence of increasing returns to scale and limited size of markets) or inherited from the state-monopoly regime of the pre-transition period.

Finally, there has been an inclination - very understandable given the preceding history of extreme inefficiency - to focus on the *efficiency* aspects *of resource allocation* while downplaying or ignoring the *distributive* aspects. Yet these latter aspects are often decisive in ensuring the political acceptability of transitional policies such as the privatization of industry, and also have at significant influence on ideological developments.

1.2 Modeling of institutions

My objective in the present chapter is to concentrate on the first issue, that is, the explicit inclusion of institutions as basic elements of economic models, and to do so at a level of generality that enables us to consider institutions as 'variables' or even 'unknowns' of the economist's problem. In treating institutions as variables we make contact with economic history and the field known as 'comparative systems'. In treating institutions as unknowns we provide a setting for systematizing the process of designing institutions.

A preliminary point to be recognized is the distinction between two meanings of the term 'institution': (A) an entity (often an organization) capable of playing the role of an economic agent (e.g., governments, academies, associations, corporations); (B) a set of principles or rules by which a system operates. We may refer to (A) as *institutional entities*, while (B) are commonly termed *institutional arrangements*. My focus is on (B), the institutional arrangements.

D.C. North (1990) refers to (A), the institutional entities, as players, and to (B), institutional arrangements, as the *rules of the game*. For some time, my approach has been to interpret institutional arrangements not just metaphorically, but as actual rules of the game, using the formal game-theoretic framework. This makes institutions accessible to analytical study and enables us to draw on the wealth of existing knowledge about properties of games of strategy. To simplify exposition we shall confine ourselves to *non-cooperative game models*, although there would be no difficulty in accommodating cooperative games within our framework.

However, the concept of a non-cooperative game by itself is insufficient for modeling institutional arrangements. Indeed, it is inadequate for distinguishing between rules of the game and the payoff functions which depend on the players' preferences. This difficulty is resolved by decomposing the payoff function of a game into its two constituent elements: (a) the so-called *game-form*, and (b) the *utility function* representing the players' preferences. In much of the economics literature the game-form is referred to as the *mechanism*. The game-form contains two elements: the players' *strategy domains* and the *outcome function*. (In the present paper I shall largely confine myself to normal form, as distinct from the extensive form, games.)

The game-form is a formalization of the rules of the game. Strategy domains define the actions (moves, strategies) that are available to the players, sometimes called 'legal', while the outcome function specifies the consequences of strategic choices made by the players. The consequences are not meant in terms of utility values but of physical outcomes such as resource allocations. By contrast, a player's *payoff function* specifies the consequences (numerically, in utility terms) to that player of choices made by *all* players. Thus a player's payoff associated with a particular set of choices made by all players represents that player's utility level associated with the physical outcomes due to those choices.

This decomposition of a payoff function into utility and outcome functions is central to the task of modeling institutional change, in particular for modeling transition, which is a movement from one institutional arrangement to another. This is so because institutional change involves a change in the game-form, but not necessarily any change in the players' preferences.

It might seem that an institutional arrangement (institution in sense (B)) should be represented by a specific game-form. But this would be too narrow. The reason can be illustrated by considering the institutional arrangement known as *sharecropping*. The outcome function of the game-form must specify the numerical ratio, say 2:3, according to which crops are divided between the landlord and the laborer. The ratio 1:1 defines a different game-form. But the common notion of sharecropping covers both these game-forms as belonging to the same institutional arrangement. Thus, it is natural to view the institution of share-cropping as including arrangements where crops are divided between the landlord and the laborer, whatever the ratio. But that means that the institution of sharecropping contains all division arrangements with ratios ranging, say, from zero to one, each represented by a game-form corresponding to a particular division ratio.

In my formalization, therefore, an institutional arrangement (institution in sense (B)) is represented by *a class of game-forms* having some significant features in common, rather than by a single game-form.

1.3 A model

Because of the unavoidable ambiguity of the preceding verbal formulation, we introduce some notation and define the concepts with the help of the notation.

There are N players. The i-th player's strategy domain is denoted by S^i, with i ranging from 1 to N. That is, player i is permitted to select his/her strategy s_i from the set S^i. The i-th player's payoff $\pi^i(s_1,\ldots,s_N)$ represents the (numerical) utility of player i when the players' strategy choices are respectively $s_1,s_2,\ldots,s_N$. With the N-list [or N-tuple] $(s_1,s_2,\ldots,s_N)$ abbreviated as s, the i-th player's payoff is written $\pi^i(s)$. Hence, π^i is a real-valued function whose domain is the *joint strategy space* $S = S^1 \times S^2 \times \ldots \times S^N$, symbolically, π^i: $S \to \mathbf{R}$, where $\mathbf{R}$ represents the set of real numbers. A *game* is defined by the joint strategy space S and an N-list $(\pi^1,\ldots,\pi^N)$ of payoff functions, while a *game-form* is defined by S and the outcome function h, to be described.

The physical outcome of the game (for example, the resulting resource allocation) is an element z of the *outcome space Z*. The *outcome function h* specifies the outcome z resulting from choices $s_1,s_2,\ldots,s_N$. This is written as $z = h(s)$, and h: $S \to Z$. In turn, the i-th player's utility function u^i associates a real number, say r_i, with a point z of the outcome space, so that $r_i = u^i(z)$ and u^i: $Z \to \mathbf{R}$. Thus, r_i is a measure of the level of satisfaction experienced by player i when the physical outcome is z.

We are now in a position to relate the payoff functions to the outcome function. Given the strategy choices $s = (s_1,s_2,\ldots,s_N)$ made by the N players, the physical outcome is $z = h(s)$. The i-th player's resulting utility is the number $r^i = u^i(z) = u^i(h(s))$. But the number r^i is precisely the i-th payoff associated with the strategy N-list s, that is, $r^i = \pi^i(s)$. Hence the

i-th payoff function is the *composition* of the outcome function with the i-th utility function. Thus,

$$\pi^1(s_1,\ldots,s_2) = u^i(h(s_1,\ldots,s_2)), \quad i = 1,2,\ldots, N,$$

and

$$\pi^i = u^i \, 0h, \quad i = 1,\ldots, N.$$

Here, the symbol '0' denotes the composition of functions.

The distinction between a *game-form* (S,h) and the game $(S,\pi^1,\ldots,\pi^N)$ is crucial for the modeling of institutional arrangements. If we think of institutional arrangements as rules of the (economic) game, these cannot be represented by the payoff functions, since the payoff functions depend on attitudes and preferences, as well as on the prevailing rules. The rules themselves are indeed represented by the game-forms. The individual strategy domains S^i (which are contained in S) indirectly specify which actions ('moves') are permitted or obligatory, while the outcome function tells us the consequences of these actions. Institutional change involves changes either in the strategy domains or in the outcome functions. It need not involve changes in utility functions.

1.4 Some consequences: from land tenure to post-socialist transformation

While it is tempting to identify the notion of an institution with a game form, such a definition turns out to be too narrow. Consider, for example, the Stiglitz model of alternative land tenure institutions: wage labor, renting, and sharecropping.

As noted by Stiglitz (1974), the respective outcome functions characterizing these three institutional arrangements are special cases of a broader class of functions in which the cultivator's (worker's) reward is defined by the reward function $r=ay+b$, where y is the crop (or value added), r the worker's reward, and a and b numerical parameters. Wage-labor is a special case with $a=0$ and b being a positive number (wage); renting is another special case, with $a=1$ and b a negative number (the rental payment); sharecropping again is a special case with $b=0$ and a being a positive number between zero and one.

To define a game-form, say for the sharecropping case, we must specify the numerical value of the parameter a. Different values of a define different game forms because the outcome functions differ. However, the qualitative aspects of the arrangement remain the same. Therefore, as long as (in the general reward formula) we have $b=0$, it is natural to consider that we are dealing with the same institution, that of sharecropping, whatever the value of a. Hence, the institution of sharecropping corresponds not to a single game-form but to a *class of game-forms* that have certain qualitative characteristics in common. Within the class of reward functions $r=ay+b$ the institution of sharecropping is defined by the subclass of game-forms satisfying the relations $b=0$ and $0<a<1$.

This example, and many like it, lead me to define an institution (in the sense of an institutional arrangement) as a class of game-forms, provided this class satisfies certain requirements, to be discussed below.

There is, of course, a great deal of flexibility and even arbitrariness in drawing boundaries of distinct institutions, which naturally depends on the problem at hand. But the proposed formulation seems to me to be particularly appropriate for discussing problems of transition which, by definition, involve a change from one type of institutional arrangement to another.

When we discuss the merits of markets versus central planning, we are thinking of the whole family of market structures (containing a variety of alternative mechanisms, that is, game-forms) as constituting a single institution, contrasted with the whole family of centralized planning structures (also containing a variety of mechanisms, that is, game-forms) constituting another institution.

In other contexts we may prefer a finer classification and split the various market mechanisms into several distinct institutional arrangements (e.g., monopoly, competition, etc.), and similarly with planning.

Viewing institutional arrangements as (classes of) game-forms has an important implication: it makes them amenable to analytical treatment by existing techniques, those of message processes (adjustment processes) and of game theory. This includes the techniques of economic mechanism design and the theory of implementation (in Maskin's sense of this term). It also includes results from the theory of message processes, such as Calsamiglia's theorem implying that, in general, Pareto-optimal allocations cannot be achieved by mechanisms using finite-dimensional message spaces. Decentralized message exchange equilibria include, in particular, Nash equilibria. Hence impossibility results for decentralized message exchange processes apply to (game-form) mechanisms, including decentralized market mechanisms. This high degree of generality of impossibility results dealing with broad classes of message exchange processes (which include many familiar economic mechanisms) is to be contrasted with results implying the impossibility of a particular mechanism, for instance the very important non-convexity results due to

Starrett (1972), implying the non-existence of competitive equilibria in economies with detrimental externalities.

While institutional arrangements are modeled as classes of game-forms, not every class of game-forms qualifies as a model of an institutional arrangement. Without claiming to be exhaustive, we shall name some of the most important characteristics that distinguish institutional game-forms from others. Readers familiar with the literature will note that these characteristics are closely related to those stressed by Schotter (1981) and Ostrom (1986).

To begin with, the institutional arrangements are *generated by human actions*. These actions may consciously aim at prescribing or prohibiting certain forms of behavior (taking, for instance, the form of legislation), but they may also be the result of custom and tradition formation over extended periods. That institutions are human creations may seem obvious. But since a game-form specifies the consequences of actions of the participants, it will in general include consequences due to the laws of physics, and so on, and not just social dictates.

Secondly, the rules specified by a game-form should be applicable to a category of situations, persons..., and not just to a particular person, action, or point in time. We refer to this feature as *categoricity*. Schotter (1981: 11) requires that an institution should specify behavior in *recurrent* situations; I view recurrence as a special aspect of categoricity.

And third, these rules should either be internalized by members of society or provided with an implementation or enforcement mechanism. In this context, the term 'implementation' differs from Maskin's usage. Thus an institutional arrangement such as social security includes not only enforceable sanctions (for example, penalties) but also apparatus for gathering required information, collecting taxes, and making payments to beneficiaries. An important implication is that, contrary to some existing views (see North, 1990: 3), institutions do not always impose constraints and need not always limit the participants' domain of action; they may in fact increase the area of freedom, at least for parts of society. Schotter (1981: 11) requires that an institution be 'either self-policed or policed by some external authority'. Such internal or external enforcement is narrower than, although covered by, the notion of implementation introduced here. For short, we call this feature *implementation*, sometimes called '*genuine implementation*', to distinguish it from Maskin's use of the term 'implementation' which refers to designing a mechanism rather than making sure that the rules can be actually put in effect and enforced, see also Hurwicz (1993). In what follows, implementation is understood to be 'genuine'.

1.5 The law

The preceding statement of characteristics is quite informal. The problem is how to translate them into formalized models suitable for analytical treatment. Consider, in particular, the way in which institutions (in the sense of institutional arrangements) are generated by human actions. As an illustration, we may use the legislative process. We shall use for this case a model patterned after that constructed by Reiter and Hughes (1981). The institution they had in mind was the set of regulations such as the anti-trust laws. These can be viewed as circumscribing what is permissible in the 'game' played by various business enterprises (that may be competing or colluding), and the agencies administering and enforcing the laws: the Department of Justice, the courts,... Since the model will involve more than one game, let me call this game (with enterprises, administrators and enforcers as players) the *substantive game*. The outcome space of this game consists of alternative resource allocations, including the specification of prices, inputs, outputs, and so on. The anti-trust laws are enacted by a legislative body, here the US Congress. But the laws passed by Congress are rather general in nature and cannot be regarded as the complete rules governing the substantive game. The rules are made complete (or, at least, more complete) by detailed regulations promulgated by various administrative bodies as well as by the courts' jurisprudence. Let us suppose that administrative regulations and jurisprudence define the rules of the substantive game, that is, a particular game-form for the substantive game. Since the regulations and jurisprudence must be consistent with the laws, one can view the laws as defining a *class* of game-forms permissible for the substantive game. In fact, this class of game-forms constitutes the anti-trust institutional arrangements. This example illustrates our notion of institutions as classes of game-forms. But how were the anti-trust institutional arrangements created?

In the Reiter-Hughes model the rule creation process is also modeled as a game. The players here are the legislators (perhaps together with lobbyists). What is special about this *legislative game* is the nature of its 'outcome space'. Since the outcome consists of anti-trust laws, the outcome space of the legislative game consists of rules for the substantive game. More formally, an element of the outcome space of the legislative game is a set of game-forms (rules) that may govern the substantive game. Since the game-form of the substantive game determines the incentive structure for that game's participants, the outcome of the legislative game can be interpreted as imposing limits on the incentive structures chosen for the substantive game by the intermediate (for instance, administrative or judicial) stages.

As a first stage of our analysis, suppose for the moment that the law specifies the rules completely and hence there is no need or room for an intermediate stage (although we know this is not typically the case). Formally then, each element of the outcome space would consist of a single game-form for the substantive game. In this case, we have a two-stage process consisting of the legislative game completely defining the rules governing the substantive game, followed by the substantive game in which the economic resource allocation will be determined.

More realistically, though, suppose that the law does not completely specify the rules of the substantive game, but that the rules are made specific by the regulations adopted by the administrative agencies within limits defined by the legislation. (We ignore here the very real possibility that those implementing or interpreting the laws may in fact go against legislative intent.) In this case we have a *three-stage process*: legislative, administrative, and substantive. In general, we might have a sequence of stages, each modeled as a game, each providing a higher degree of specificity with respect to substantive game rules. We refer to such a sequence as a *cascade*, see Hurwicz (1996 a,b). The Reiter-Hughes model is a two-stage cascade. It has the additional feature that the legislative stage is modeled as a cooperative game, while the substantive stage is non-cooperative. But these features need not always be present.

When institutions develop as a result of slow processes, such as custom formation, alternative models may be more appropriate. Schotter's use of a super-game may be a step in this direction.

Returning to the example of a multi-stage cascade consisting of legislative, intermediate, and substantive stages, a crucial problem is that of ('genuine') *implementation*. If the rules have not been internalized, why would players in the substantive game obey the rules promulgated by law?

Before we proceed to deal with this question, let us note an occasionally heard objection, to the effect that a Nash equilibrium is self-enforcing, presumably because - by the definition of Nash equilibrium - a unilateral departure from his/her ('legal') Nash strategy domain, here denoted S^{i*}, cannot benefit the player. (The asterisk indicates reference to the prescribed - 'legal' - game-form.) This may seem to imply that if Nash equilibrium is used as the solution concept, the problem of enforcement does not arise. But the claim of the 'self-enforcing' feature of a Nash equilibrium is based on the implicit premise that the rules of the game are being observed. That is, that no player uses 'illegal' strategies and (very important!) that there is apparatus in place ensuring that the outcome resulting from the N-tuple of $(s_1,\ldots,s_N)$ strategies chosen by the players is that prescribed by the game-form's outcome function, that is,

$h^*(s_1,...,s)$. But it is the premise that the rules are being observed that is at issue here. The need for enforcement apparatus arises precisely from the possibility that some players might find it to their advantage to violate these rules. And when that happens, the 'self-enforcement' claim for Nash equilibria is no longer valid. Note that even when players use legal strategies, the outcome may be different from the prescribed outcome $h^*(s)$ because of lack of the required implementation apparatus.

The obvious answer is to assume that there exists some implementation (enforcement) apparatus. But even then, some players may adopt behavior violating the law's rules, presumably incurring, or at least risking, some sanctions. How do we model this phenomenon? It is not enough to consider the game-form where the substantive strategy domains are those declared permissible (according to laws, regulations and jurisprudence), say S^{1*},..., S^{N*}, where 1,..., N are the players in the substantive game (including the enforcers!). We must also consider *all* the feasible illegal behaviors, say T^1, ..., T^N of these players. We call the game-form recognizing illegal as well as legal strategies and also admitting the possibility of imperfect implementation an *augmented game-form* (because it is much larger than the game-form that only recognizes the legal strategies).

This model is, in my opinion, not open to the criticism of 'infinite regress' because an augmented game-form is, in a sense, *maximal*: it takes into account the consequences of *all feasible* configurations of legal and illegal behavior (assuming that there is no grey area between legal and illegal). This does not imply, however, that, even in principle, every designed legal game-form can in fact be implemented. One can imagine a situation where even those charged with the implementation are corrupt and the rules of the game as legislated are not and cannot be enforced. Analytically, this means that the equilibrium outcome of the augmented game is not an equilibrium of the prescribed (legal) game, or perhaps that the augmented game does not have an equilibrium point.

Because the augmented game-form recognizes all possible behaviors and takes into account the imperfections of implementation, it is more realistic than the more usual models postulating legal behavior and perfect implementation.

In the augmented game-form, the *i*-th player's strategy space can be written as a pair (S^{i*}, T^i), where T^i is the illegal component. The 'realistic' outcome functions of the augmented game-form will be denoted by h, as distinct from the prescribed outcome functions h^*. The augmented outcome function's operation is symbolized by h: $(S^*, T) \rightarrow \mathbf{R}$. Its values may differ from the prescribed ones even when the strategies chosen are legal. Thus, it may happen that, due to imperfect implementation apparatus, $h(s) \neq h^*(s)$ even when s is an element of the legal joint strategy space S^*.

Formally then, the *augmented game-form* can be written as an N-list of such strategy pairs combined with the realistic (as distinct from prescribed) outcome function, that is, as $<(S^{1*},T^1),...,(S^{N*},T^N); h>$ where the i-th player's strategy space consists of the elements of both S^{i*} and T^i, that is, both legal and illegal behavior, and the consequences of the players' chosen actions, as defined by $h : (S^*, T) \rightarrow \mathbf{R}$.

Unless the rules have been internalized, the actual outcome will be the Nash equilibrium of the augmented - rather than the legal - game, that is, the game defined by the composition of the agents' preferences with the augmented game-form.

To analyze this augmented game we must know not only what happens when players behave legally, and implementation is complete, that is - know the values of the prescribed outcome function $h^*(s)$ with s in the legal domain S^*, but also know what happens if one or more players choose illegal strategies, for instance, the outcome is $h(t_1,...,t_N)$ where everybody uses an illegal strategy, and h is the function describing the consequences of such behavior.

To clarify the concept of an augmented game matrix, consider a simple case of a two-player game (N=2), and suppose that the strategy domains are finite, with the legal domain S^{i*} of the i-th player consisting of m_i legal strategies and T^i consisting of k_i illegal strategies, i=1,2. Then the augmented outcome function is defined by a matrix with, say m_1+k_1 rows and m_2+k_2 columns. It can be partitioned into four submatrices. The upper left m_1 by m_2 submatrix specifies outcomes $h(s_1,s_2)$ when both players use legal strategies (this outcome may still be different from the prescribed $h^*(s_1,s_2)$); the lower right k_1 by k_2 submatrix specifies the outcomes $h(t_1,t_2)$ when both players use illegal strategies; the lower left k_1 by m_2 submatrix specifies the outcomes $h(t_1,s_2)$ when player 1 uses illegal strategies while player 2 uses legal strategies; finally the m_1 by k_2 upper right submatrix specifies the outcomes $h(s_1,t_2)$ with player 1 playing legal strategies and player 2 illegal ones.

As noted above, due to illegal behavior and/or imperfect implementation, the actual outcomes may differ from the prescribed ones. This is a classical question: who will guard the guardians? '... sed quis custodiet ipsos custodes?', Juvenalis, *Liber Secundus, Satura VI*, lines 347-8, p. 325.

But it is a fact that there are societies and periods where many, perhaps most, 'rules of the game' are reasonably well implemented and corruption is not widespread. One of the fundamental questions of institutional design is to develop an understanding of what accounts for the difference between the two types of situations. The issue has been treated by the author elsewhere in some detail (Hurwicz, 1993).

Clearly, there are interactions over time between the prevailing institutions and the *economic environment* (that is, economic characteristics such as resource endowments, available technologies, preferences and prevailing attitudes). The characteristics determine to a considerable extent which institutional arrangements can and are likely to be adopted. On the other hand the prevailing institutional arrangements affect incentive structures and hence rates of economic growth and other economic variables. This interplay has been interpreted in a dynamic model constructed by Reiter and Hughes.

1.6 Some conclusions

The 1980s and 1990s have been years of remarkable institutional changes, mostly from planned or centralized economies to market economies and relaxed regulations. Of necessity, the results have been mixed systems, while the discussion - especially in some of the formerly 'socialist' countries - has sometimes tended to focus on the benefits of transition to the idealized perfectly competitive markets. It is therefore important to keep in mind the limitations of even the perfectly competitive (Walrasian) model.

A basic postulate underlying the perfectly competitive model is that economic agents ignore any influence their actions might have on the state of the market, specifically on prices. This, however, is less likely to be true in 'thin' markets, where the number of buyers or sellers is low (actually or potentially). In such cases it is more realistic to expect imperfect competition, oligopoly or oligopsony, or even monopoly/ monopsony.

In addition, various circumstances may rule out even the *logical* possibility of existence of a competitive equilibrium, namely, of prices balancing demand and supply in all markets simultaneously. The most important of such situations is the presence of increasing returns to scale (decreasing average costs, 'natural monopoly'), a phenomenon of particular importance in developing younger economies. None of the remedies used or proposed for such situations (regulation, state ownership, subsidized marginal cost pricing) have proved completely satisfactory, even in theory. In fact, there are theoretical results (see Calsamiglia, 1977) implying that a first best decentralized mechanism guaranteeing efficiency in such situations would require infinite information transfers.

What makes the notion of competitive equilibrium so attractive is the classic First Theorem of Welfare Economics, asserting that, under certain assumptions, the main ones being finite time horizons and absence of externalities, the competitive equilibrium resource allocations (if not logically ruled out as under increasing returns) are bound to be efficient (Pareto optimal). But the theorem fails to hold in the presence of externalities or over infinite time horizons. Again, recent theoretical work leads to the conclusion that, with finite information processing capacity, first best efficiency cannot be guaranteed by any decentralized mechanism. In an era where environmental degradation (due to pollution, a classic detrimental externality) is a worldwide issue, these results must be taken very seriously.

These considerations do not imply that markets are inferior to alternative institutional arrangements, but rather that they have their limitations. We may have to be reconciled to 'second best' outcomes and to mechanisms that use the most efficient features of markets together with non-market elements where unavoidable or appropriate. This view is strengthened by bearing in mind that economic systems are judged not only on their efficiency aspects, but also on other criteria - in particular, how they affect the situation of the weaker social elements and the degree of economic inequality.

References

Calsamiglia, X. (1977) Decentralized Resource Allocation and Increasing Returns. *Journal of Economic Theory*, **14**, 263-83.

Hurwicz, L. (1993) Implementation and Enforcement in Institutional Modeling. Chapter 2 in: W. A. Barnett, M. J. Hinich and N. J. Schofield, eds. *Political Economy, Institutions, Competition and Representation.* Cambridge: Cambridge University Press, 51-59.

Hurwicz, L. (1996a) Institutions as Families of Game Forms. *The Japanese Economic Review*, **47,** 113-32.

Hurwicz, L. (1996b) Economic Design, Adjustment Processes, Mechanisms and Institutions. *Economic Design*, **1**, 1-14.

Juvenal (1985) *D. Junii Juvenalis Saturarum Libri V.* Leipzig: Verlag von S. Hirzel.

North, D.C. (1990) *Institutions, Institutional Change, and Economic Performance.* Cambridge: Cambridge University Press.

Ostrom, E. (1986) An agenda for the Study of Institutions. *Public Choice*, **48**, 3-25.

Reiter, S. and J. Hughes (1981) A preface on Modeling the Regulated United States Economy. *Hofstra Law Review*, **9**, 1381-21.

Schotter, A. (1981) *The Economic Theory of Social Institutions.* Cambridge: Cambridge University Press.

Starrett, D. (1972) Fundamental Nonconvexities in the Theory of Externalities. *Journal of Economic Theory*, **4**, 180-99.

Stiglitz, J. (1974) Incentives in Risk Sharing and Sharecropping. *Review of Economic Studies*, **41**, 219-56.

Chapter 2

When do Stakes in Restructuring put Restructuring at Stake?

Philipp J.H. Schröder

Frequently the shareholders of privatized transition firms also hold stakes in the firm they own. This two-sided role of an agent may give rise to potential conflicts when the restructuring strategy of a firm has to be decided. This shareholder/stakeholder conflict is analyzed in a simple framework including the corporate control dimension of the problem. It is found that for feasible specifications of the conflict, restructuring in the economy will fall short of complete efficiency. However, for certain parameter values the shareholder/stakeholder issue turns out to be a non-problem.
The author wishes to thank Stephen Pudney, Peter Skott, Alf Vanags and Ebbe Yndgaard for valuable discussions. The usual disclaimer applies.

2.1 Introduction

This chapter formalizes the conflict between shareholder and stakeholder interests in transition economies. While extensive privatization programs have emerged in all of the transition economies, restructuring - the elimination of inefficiencies - has often been absent. For a recent and comprehensive overview on restructuring in transition see Djankov and Murrell (2002), who examine, by means of meta-analysis, inter alia, the effects of privatization, the role of different types of owners, etc. for enterprise restructuring. For example, when controlling for regional differences, their analysis finds no evidence of a different impact from either worker or manager owners on restructuring in CEE enterprises, i.e. a finding that could be explained within the present stakeholder/ shareholder framework. Earlier surveys repeatedly found similar results. We observe that employment is reduced by less than output. Overmanning prevails in many firms, e.g. Aghion and Carlin (1996), Commander, Dhar and Yemtsov (1996). Enterprises continue to provide a host of social services and assets for the benefits of their workers, see e.g. Freinkman and Starodubrovskaya (1996), Commander and Schankerman

(1997). Recently Earle and Estrin (2003) have re-examined the early impact of privatization in Russia.

Overall, it appears that - contrary to common belief - privatization by itself does not warrant restructuring. The literature has identified several channels and inherent design faults in privatization programs that contribute to a lack of (or incomplete) restructuring; see, for example, Brada (1996), Nuti (1997a, 1997b), Aghion and Blanchard (1996, 1998), Filatochev *et al.* (1999a, 1999b), Roland and Sekkat (2000), Schröder (2001, 2003), Djankov and Murrell (2002), Earle and Estrin (2003) Filatochev *et al.* (2003).

The argument of the present chapter starts with the observation, that frequently the new owners of privatized State Owned Enterprises (SOEs) hold not only shares but also stakes in the same firm. For a debate about the involved benefits and problems see Nuti (1998). The two-sided role of an agent, as both a shareholder and a stakeholder, gives rise to potential conflicts. Stakes in firms and in firms' inefficiencies can be of various kinds. Agents may be suppliers of labour or other inputs, debtors or creditors, beneficiaries of firm social assets, distributors of firm output, leaseholders of firm assets, etc. Having such a stake in a firm (apart from a share in equity) may bias an agent to hinder restructuring, since certain inefficiencies in the firm (say idle labour) - that a shareholder would want to eliminate - may in fact benefit the agent that is also a stakeholder. That such stakeholder issues create problems in privatizations and have potentially harmful effects on restructuring has been pointed out by among other Bolton and Roland (1992), Aghion and Burgess (1994), Nuti (1997a, 1997b) and Cauley *et al.* (1999). Other have argued - partly in line with the present chapter - that stakeholdings and insider shareholdings need not create a problem, see, for example, the contribution of Kuznetsova and Kuznetsov (2001) and their assessment of the Russian case. Also of importance for the debate, but not the object of this paper are socioeconomic approaches to these types of problems, see, for example, Wright and Mukherji (1999).

The common version of the shareholder/stakeholder conflicts is that shareholder/stakeholder setups will turn into a problem once an individual holds a smaller share in equity than in the total stake, e.g. the total input supplied, benefits received, idle work hours, assets stripped, etc. Such as imbalance implies that the agent's stakeholder interests could override their shareholder interests. The typical example is the firm's workforce. The workers might only hold part of the equity share in their firm, but receive all wage expenditure of the firm, hence workers will - ceteris paribus - in a shareholder meeting vote for wage increases.

Related to this one can consider the role of managerial career concerns during transition, e.g. Dyck (1997), Roland and Sekkat (2000), Schröder (2003).

The point that agents stakeholder interests could override their shareholder interests, was in the context of transition, first made explicitly by Nuti (1997a, 1997b). However, the discussion of stakeholder/ shareholder conflicts has also addressed the underlying corporate control issue. The common version of the shareholder/stakeholder conflict argues that too small a share in equity could cause an agent to follow his stakeholder interests (which may be anti-restructuring), when deciding on the firm's restructuring policy. But a small share in equity, in fact, reduces the individual's influence on corporate control, such that his preferences matter less for the eventual firm strategy adopted! Hence, it is not entirely obvious that stakeholder interests can actually hinder restructuring. In a simple linear programming framework - explicitly treating the corporate control dimension - the present contribution analyzes how, and under what conditions, conflicts between shareholder interests and stakeholder interests will actually cause failures in restructuring, and when they are harmless.

The main findings of the chapter are: (1) Allocation of shares to stakeholders will either promote or hinder restructuring dependent on the sign of their stakeholder interests (i.e. we do allow stakeholder interests to either benefit or lose from restructuring). (2) The critical relative size of equity shares and the stakeholder function are derived. (3) It is shown that the restructuring level in the economy may fall short due to the stakeholder/shareholder conflict. (4) Soft budgets will increase the inefficiency of a firm if the controlling group has a sufficiently positive stakeholder interest in inefficiency. (5) Shares held by outsiders (i.e. private citizens or foreigners) i.e. non-stakeholders, promote restructuring in the economy.

The chapter proceeds as follows: section 2 introduces the model. Section 3 analyses the restructuring decision of individual firms, whereby the firm's restructuring strategy depends crucially on the stakeholder functions of its majority shareholders. Section 4 considers the resulting restructuring level in the entire economy. Section 5 concludes the chapter.

2.2 A simple model

A government has imposed a 'give away' privatization program. Each firm $i\,(i=1...n)$ is privatized such that all shares are allocated between three types of agents. Shares are given either to two different types of stakeholders g_i (inherently pro-restructuring) and h_i (inherently anti-restructuring) and to a third type of agent, namely non-stakeholders o_i (outsiders). Stakes are only in the inefficiency, and payoff from the inefficiency can be either positive or negative, depending on the stakeholder preferences as separated by their behavioral functions $g(.)$ and $h(.)$ respectively. In particular, agents have an underlying pro- or anti-restructuring preference (dislike or like for the inefficiency). However, their action emerges after their stakeholder interest is combined with their shareholder interest. Ownership of shares is modelled by splitting the profits of firm *i* between representative agents of the three shareholder groups. With regard to corporate control we assume that control rights and hence the decision whether to restructure or not follows directly from the property rights.

Firms vary as to the allocation of shares. The agent g_i of firm *i* holds α_i shares in his firm, while agent h_i holds $1-\alpha_i$. We assume that the distribution of shares in the economy is the outcome of the privatization program that has been administered by the government. More formally, assume that α_i is distributed uniformly on [0,1]. Let $F(.)$ denote the distribution function, so that $F(0)=0$ and $F(1)=1$. This function represents the outcome of the privatization program. This tool allows us to assess the restructuring occurring in the entire economy as a result of individual firm behavior. Further, the privatization program that is administered by the government features outside owners. Formally, the amount of $(1-2\theta)$ shares in each firm is given to outsiders o_i who hold no stakes in the inefficiency ($\theta \in \left[0,\frac{1}{2}\right]$)[1]. The total amount of shares in firm *i* is thus given by $\alpha_i+(1-\alpha_i)+(1-2\theta)=2-2\theta$. Note that we implicitly assume that at least half of all the shares in a firm are with stakeholders. It will be shown that outsiders are pro-restructuring and hence always vote and agree with the decisions of the *g* agent. Hence the *g* agent of firm *i* effectively assumes corporate control once $\alpha_i>\theta$, i.e. at least θ shares in firm *i* are controlled by the *g* agent, else the *h* agent is in charge. To see why this holds, realize that the necessary amount of shares to assume corporate control must be greater than $\frac{2-2\theta}{2}=1\text{-}\theta$, i.e. half of all the shares in firm *i*. Hence, to determine when agent *g* will

---

[1] This way of introducing outside (non-stakeholder) shares is designed such that we receive a tractable control parameter θ, which turns out to be the threshold share size for agent g_i to assume corporate control in firm *i*.

be in charge we solve $\alpha_i + (1-2\theta) > 1-\theta$ which turns out as $\alpha_i > \theta$. For the h group to assume control a similar argument holds. A useful reference case will be $\theta = \frac{1}{2}$, i.e. no outside owners $(1-2\theta) = 0$ and hence 0.5 share give complete control rights to group g.

Assuming that there are no deficiency of demand issues and that capital is fixed, firms have a potential gross profit $\Pi_i + b_i$, where Π_i is the profit from fully efficient production and b_i is a transfer payment from the government. The transfer represents soft budget constraints, and is activated in case of illiquidity: or - in a slight abuse of terminology - called bankruptcy. The removal of soft budget constraints is still an issue in many transition countries, e.g. Kornai (2001), Brücker et al. (2005). The joint gross profit to agent g_i and h_i - or rather gross profit per share - is given by $\pi_i = \frac{\Pi_i + b_i}{2-2\theta}$.

Firms start out with some inefficiency. In particular, firm i has an amount of inefficiency Λ_i at a cost w. The inefficiency is covered out of $(\Pi_i + b_i)$, and the gross loss due to inefficiency for group g and h in firm i is given by $wL_i = \frac{w\Lambda_i}{2-2\theta}$. Accordingly, overall net profits of firm i are given by $(\Pi_i + b_i - w\Lambda_i)$, while net profits to the agents of group g and h are given by $(\pi_i - wL_i)$. To simplify the analysis and without loss of generality we assume that a fraction $\frac{1-2\theta}{2-2\theta}$ of the total inefficiency Λ_i is pure waste, which does not enter the stakeholder functions. Hence, we get stakeholder functions $g(L_i,...)$ and $h(L_i,...)$ assumed to be linear in L_i. Such specification of inefficiencies relates to Shleifer and Vishny (1994); in their model L_i is the number of extra (idle) workers. In the present model L_i could also represent other forms of inefficiency that may reduce company profits: the number of idle worker hours, units of excessive social benefits, amount of asset stripping, sub-optimal leasehold contracts, extension of inter-enterprise arrears, etc. Thus, restructuring means to cut down Λ_i or equivalently L_i.

Denoting by $\bar{b}$ the upper limit of transfers to the firm, the soft budget constraint b_i can be defined as:

$$b_i = \begin{cases} 0 & \text{if } \Pi_i - w\Lambda_i > 0 \\ Min\{w\Lambda_i - \Pi_i, \bar{b}\} & \text{if } \Pi_i - w\Lambda_i < 0 \end{cases}$$

Consider the preferences of the different types of agents. The utility function of the representative h shareholder (anti-restructuring) is in its open version given by $U_{h_i} = H((1-\alpha_i), \pi_i, L_i, w)$, i.e. depending on his share in the firm, gross profit and inefficiency. We postulate the specific utility function of the h agent in firm i to be given by:

$$U_{h_i} = (1-\alpha_i)(\pi_i - wL_i) + h(L_i). \quad (2.1)$$

The h agent cares about the dividend on his shares $(1-\alpha_i)$, paid out of net profits. This represents his shareholder interest. His stakeholder interests are represented by the stakeholder function $h(L_i)$, where $h'(L_i)$, is constant and $h'(L_i) > 0$.

We proceed to postulate an agent g type utility function (pro restructuring), which in its open version will be of the form $U_{g_i} = G(\alpha_i, \pi_i, L_i, w)$.

The specific form of U_{g_i} is assumed to be:

$$U_{g_i} = \alpha_i(\pi_i - wL_i) + g(L_i). \quad (2.2)$$

The g type cares about the dividend on his shares, i.e. his shareholder interests. The function $g(L_i)$ represents his stakeholder interest in the inefficiency L_i where $g'(L_i) < 0$ and is constant. For example, the $g-$agent could be a firm manager, who increases his market value if the firm he runs has a high level of efficiency, hence he has a negative stake in the inefficiency. Having introduced the functions U_{h_i} and U_{g_i}, it should become obvious that the following analysis is concerned with the resulting sign of $\frac{dU_{g_i}}{dL_i}$ and $\frac{dU_{h_i}}{dL_i}$ respectively. For completeness we define the utility function of outsiders (no stakes) as $U_{o_i} = (1-2\theta)\frac{(\Pi_i + b_i - w\Lambda_i)}{(2-2\theta)}$. Thus, when maximizing U_{o_i} it turns out that outsiders will always vote for $\Lambda_i = 0$ or equivalently $L_i = 0$, i.e. pure profit maximization.

Further we require that the companies' net profits are semi positive and that efficiency can only be obtained to the degree of $\Lambda_i = 0$ and not beyond. Hence:

$$(\pi_i - wL_i) \geq 0 \quad (2.3)$$

$$L_i \geq 0. \quad (2.4)$$

Henceforth we call (2.3) for the liquidity constraint implicitly assuming that there are no capital markets where firms can loan. We are now able to state our first result.

Proposition 1

The inefficiency level in firm i is restricted by $L_i \in [0, \frac{\pi_i}{w}|_{b_i = \bar{b}}]$. *The maximum possible degree of inefficiency for firm i rises with an increase in the upper limit of soft budgets* $\bar{b}$.

The proposition follows from (2.3) and (2.4) and the fact that π_i rises in $\bar{b}$. Hence, the possible inefficiency found in a firm *i* is bounded by the liquidity constraint and the non-negativity constraint; further, soft budgets increase the maximum possible inefficiency level in a firm.

In both utility functions (2.1) and (2.2) the choice variable is L_i, i.e. the amount of inefficiency (excess labour or social assets, use of inter-enterprise arrears, asset stripping, etc.) accepted in a particular firm *i*. Our model boils down to a linear programming problem. The maximand and the constraints of our problem change for different firms, depending on L_i, since the control rights change with L_i being greater or less than θ. In particular, if $L_i > \theta$, then we maximize U_{g_i} subject to (2.3) and (2.4); while for a company $L_i < \theta$, we maximize U_{h_i} subject to (2.3) and (2.4).

The present model is of a simple static form. However it allows a detailed analysis of the effect of the shareholder/stakeholder conflict on the amount of inefficiency chosen by different owner groups and hence the level of restructuring in the economy. The model takes a snapshot of the restructuring incentives of different shareholders after a privatization program is administered. The tractability of this setup allows us to define precisely under what conditions stakeholder interests may overrule shareholder interests in such a way as to actually alter the firm's restructuring decision.

2.3 Restructuring decisions of individual firms

It is now possible to analyse the restructuring behaviour of different firms in the economy. We distinguish between two different cases, depending on whether agent *h* or *g* assumes control. However, the entire economy will be composed of both cases - types of firms - as a result of the privatization program.

We start by considering firms were the controlling agent is a g type stakeholder. Formally we consider the case of a firm where $\alpha_i > \theta$. Using equations (2.1) to (2.4) we find our problem to be given by:

$$\begin{aligned} \max_{L_i} U_{g_i} &= \alpha_i(\pi_i - wL_i) + g(L_i) \\ s.t. \quad & (\pi_i - wL_i) \geq 0, \end{aligned}$$

and the non-negativity constraint $\alpha_i \geq 0$. The solution must be found in the range $[0, \frac{\pi_i}{w}|_{b_i=\bar{b}}]$ (which follows from Proposition 1). Given the linearity of the setup, the problem is restricted to corner solutions. Hence, there are only two possible levels of inefficiency (L_i^a and L_i^b) that can be a solution to the agent g maximization problem. By Proposition 1, the two points are $L_i^a = 0$ and $L_i^b = \frac{\pi_i}{w}|_{b_i - \bar{b}} = \frac{\Pi + \bar{b}}{w(2-2\theta)}$. What inefficiency level is chosen by agent g depends now on (2), in particular, it depends on the slope of the utility function:

$$L_i = \begin{cases} 0 & \text{if } U'_{g_i} < 0 \\ \dfrac{\Pi + \bar{b}}{w(2-2\theta)} & \text{if } U'_{g_i} > 0 \end{cases}. \tag{2.5}$$

Evaluating the slope of (2.2) by differentiating with respect to L_i we get:

$$U'_{g_i} = -\alpha_i w + g'(L_i) < 0. \tag{2.6}$$

It is now possible to define the restructuring decision of firms controlled by g agents.

Proposition 2

Agent g in firm i has always solution L_i^a - complete restructuring - as his maximizing choice.

This result follows straight from (2.5) and (2.6). Notice that the g agent will - independent of his equity shares - always vote for complete restructuring, i.e. reducing inefficiency to zero.

We can now consider the slightly more complicated case where the h agent (characterized by the like of the inefficiency) is in control of the firm. Formally, we analyze the case where $\alpha_i < \theta$. Using equations (2.1) to (2.4) our problem can be stated as:

$$\max_{L_i} U_{h_i} = (1-\alpha_i)(\pi_i - wL_i) + h(L_i)$$
$$s.t. \quad (\pi_i - wL_i) \geq 0,$$

and the non-negativity constraint $L_i \geq 0$. Evoking Proposition 1 we have again two possible levels of inefficiency (L_i^a and L_i^b) that can be a solution to the agent *h* maximization problem. Hence, the agent's choice turns out to be parallel to (2.5). Whether the upper or the lower corner solution is the maximizing inefficiency level for agent *h* depends on the derivative of (2.1). Differentiating with respect to L_i yields:

$$U'_{h_i} = (\alpha_i - 1)w + h'(L_i). \tag{2.7}$$

Since $h'(L_i) > 0$ the sign of (2.7) can be positive or negative. This gives rise to the following result:

Proposition 3
The inefficiency choice of an agent h controlled firm i is given by

$$L_i = \begin{cases} 0 & if\ (1-\alpha_i) > \dfrac{h'(L_i)}{w} \\ \dfrac{\Pi + \overline{b}}{w(2-2\theta)} & f\ (1-\alpha_i) < \dfrac{h'(L_i)}{w} \end{cases} . \tag{2.8}$$

The proposition says that if the share in equity is larger than the marginal gain from an extra unit of inefficiency, then *h* agents will restructure completely. On the other hand, if stakeholder interests in the inefficiency are sufficiently positive, then the share to the *h* agent might be too small to warrant restructuring and the agent opts for the upper inefficiency level. Hence a firm *i* where,

$$\theta > \alpha_i > \frac{w - h'(L_i)}{w} \tag{2.9}$$

will not be restructured due to the shareholder/stakeholder conflict. Notice how a larger share to the *h* agent might ensure restructuring. In the model, for a fall in *w* - the cost of inefficiency - the no-restructuring outcome is more likely to be the agent's maximizing choice. Proposition 3 is the general statement of the shareholder/stakeholder conflict for economic agents. The analysis of Nuti (1997a) turns out to be a special case of (2.8). Nuti determines that stake holdings are potentially threatening, once the share in equity is less than the share in the total input supplied (total stakes). The above condition refines his observation.

Inefficiency will prevail once the share in equity is less than the marginal gain (to the agent) from inefficiency.

Propositions 2 and 3 turn out to be intuitively straightforward, namely that the g agent opts for restructuring since he dislikes inefficiency as a stakeholder, and that the h agent opts for no-restructuring if he holds sufficiently positive stakes in the inefficiency, however for a very weak positive stake in the inefficiency his shareholder interests will override his stakeholder interests.

2.4 Restructuring in the economy

It is now possible to address our initial question - namely, can there be agents in control of firms (hence having substantial equity shares) who still opt for no-restructuring? Can the stakeholder/shareholder conflict actually materialize? The answer is yes. Using Propositions 2 and 3 and our definition of the distribution function ($F(.)$) of shares in the economy we can state:

Proposition 4

The economy described in Section 2 consists of:

(i) $(1-\theta)n$ *firms that are controlled by g agents and restructured;*

(ii) $\left(\theta - \frac{w-h'(L_i)}{w}\right)n$ *firms that are controlled by h agents and not restructured;*

and

(iii) $\left(\frac{w-h'(L_i)}{w}\right)n$ *firms that are controlled by h agents and restructured.*

The proposition states that the firms of type (ii) are those where the conflict actually materialized as an obstacle to restructuring, while all the firms in (iii) do actually feature anti-restructuring owners in control, however, they are equipped with sufficiently many equity shares such as to override their stakeholder interest. Firms in group (i) do always restructure, as they are controlled by pro-restructuring agents. Thus we have shown that also when taking account of the corporate control setting the shareholder/stakeholder conflict can actually materialize such that some firms in the economy will continue their inefficiencies.

Yet, from Proposition 4 it also becomes clear that there are several situations where the shareholder/stakeholder conflict turns out to be a *non-problem*! In particular, for a privatization program favoring more g

agents, for a larger cost of inefficiency (w), for a larger share to outsiders (lower θ) and for less benefit from the inefficiency (smaller $h'(L_i)$) the group of firms of type (ii) will shrink (eventually to zero), while the number of restructuring type firms (i) and (iii) will grow.

This leads to the following results. As to the role of outside owners we find: The share of h controlled firms falls as θ falls (which means an increase of outsider shares). Hence, an increased number of outside shareholders will ensure that more firms are completely restructured. In fact an increase in outsider owners ensures that more g agents are in control. Formally:

Corollary 1
Given that for some firms the condition in Proposition 4(ii) is fulfilled, then, ceteris paribus, a sufficient rise in the share to outside owners o_i would lead to more restructuring in the economy.

This result - which corresponds nicely to the stylized facts for transition economies - follows from the definition of outsider shares $o_i = (1-2\theta)$, i.e. a rise in the outsider share is defined as a fall in θ. So, for more outsiders receiving shares in a firm i, the agent g_i would eventually take control.

Similarly we can state for the role of soft budget constraints:

Corollary 2
Given that for some firms the condition in Proposition 4(ii) is fulfilled, then, ceteris paribus, an increase in the upper limit of soft budget constraints $\bar{b}$ will increase the overall inefficiency of the economy.

This corollary extends Proposition 1 and follows from the specification of L_i^b, namely, $L_i^b = \dfrac{\Pi + \bar{b}}{w(2-2\theta)}$.

2.5 Conclusion

Frequently, the shareholders of newly privatized firms in transition economies are also stakeholders in the same firm. Stakeholders that benefit from certain firm inefficiencies may, in their shareholder role, opt against restructuring. This case will occur if their share in equity is sufficiently small compared to their (positive) stake in the inefficiency. Yet, if their share in equity is small they may be able to alter the course of the firm. So it is not entirely clear if and when the shareholder/stakeholder conflict will materialize as an obstacle to restructuring. This chapter addressed this issue in a simple formal framework where mass-privatization of inefficient SOE's consists of the allocation of shares to different types of agents in society. The conflict between shareholder interests and stakeholder interests was at the centre of the analysis. It was found that for sensible versions of the shareholder/stakeholder conflict restructuring will fall short of complete efficiency. In addition to the central observation that restructuring is lagging behind, and that shareholders are often also stakeholders in the firms they own, the chapter incorporates a number of additional stylized facts into the formal model. Most importantly, the model allows for the privatization program to feature outside or foreign shareholders that by definition have no stake in the firm and includes a parameter representing soft budget constraints.

To summarize the main findings: First, the allocation of shares to agents that are also stakeholders endangers the restructuring efficiency of privatization, the precise critical values for the stakeholder interests to dominate their shareholder interests are calculated and the composition of the economy (consisting of restructured and un-restructured firms) is examined. Secondly, soft budget constraints can increase the inefficiency level in the economy. Thirdly, outside agents have a positive effect on restructuring. Overall, the chapter exemplifies how privatization programs may fail to trigger rigorous restructuring, but also that stake holdings may turn out to be a non-problem.

References

Aghion, P. and O. Blanchard (1996) On Insider Privatization. *European Economic Review*, **40**(3-4), 759-66.

Aghion, P. and O. Blanchard (1998) On Privatization Methods in Eastern Europe and their Implications. *Economics of Transition*, **6**(1), 87-99.

Aghion, P. and R. Burgess (1994) Financing in Eastern Europe and the Former Soviet Union. In: Dilip K. Das (ed.), *International Finance: Contemporary Issues*. London: Routledge.

Aghion, P. and W. Carlin (1996) Restructuring Outcomes and the Evolution of Ownership Patterns in Central and Eastern Europe. *Economics of Transition*, **4**(2), 371-88.

Bolton, P. and G. Roland (1992) Privatization policies in Central and Eastern Europe. *Economic Policy*, **15**, 276-309.

Brada, J.C. (1996) Privatisation is Transition - Or is it? *Journal of Economic Perspectives*, **10**(2), 67-86.

Brücker, H., P.J.H. Schröder, and C. Weise (2005) Can EU Conditionality Remedy Soft Budget Constraints in Transition Countries. *Journal of Comparative Economics*, **33**(2), 371-386.

Cauley, J., R. Cornes and T. Sandler (1999) Stakeholder Incentives and Reform in China's State-Owned Enterprises: A Common-Property Theory. *China Economic Review*, **10**, 191-06.

Commander, S., S. Dhar and R. Yemtsov (1996) How Russian Firms Make their Wage and Employment Decisions. In: S. Commander, Q. Fan and M.E. Schaffer (eds), *Enterprise Restructuring and Economic Policy in Russia.* Washington, DC: World Bank.

Commander, S. and M. Schankerman (1997) Enterprise Restructuring and Social Benefits. *Economics of Transition*, **5**(1), 1-24.

Djankov, S. and P. Murrell (2002) Enterprise Restructuring in Transition: A Quantitative Survey. *Journal of Economic Literature*, **40**(3), 739-92.

Dyck, I.J.A. (1997) Privatization in Eastern Germany: Management Selection and Economic Transition. *American Economic Review*, **87**(4), 565-97.

Earle, J. S. and S. Estrin (2003) Privatisation, Competition, and Budget Constraints: Disciplining Enterprises in Russia. *Economics of Planning*, **36**, 1-22.

Filatochev, I., M. Wright and M. Bleaney (1999a) Privatisation, Insider Control and Managerial Entrenchment in Russia. *Economics of Transition*, **7**(2), 481-04.

Filatochev, I., M. Bleaney, and M. Wright (1999b) Insider-Controlled Firms in Russia. *Economics of Planning*, **32**, 129-51.

Filatotchev, I., M. Wright, K. Uhlenbruck, L. Tihanyi and R.E. Hoskisson (2003) Governance, Organizational Capabilities, and Restructuring in Transition Economies. *Journal of World Business*, **38**(4), 331-47.

Freinkman, L.M. and I. Starodubrovskaya (1996) Restructuring of Enterprise Social Assets in Russia: Trends, Problems, Possible Solutions. *Communist Economies & Economic Transformation*, **8**(4), 437-469.

Kornai, J. (2001) Hardening the Budget Constraint: The Experience of the Post-socialist Countries. *European Economic Review*, **45**(4), 1573-99.

Kuznetsova, O. and A. Kuznetsov (2001) The Virtues and Weaknesses of Insider Shareholding. *Journal of East-West Business*, **6** (4), 89-106.

Nuti, D. M. (1997a) Employeeism: Corporate Governance and Employee Share Ownership in Transitional Economies. In: M.I. Blejer and M. Skreb (eds), *Macroeconomic Stabilisation in Transition Economies*. Cambridge: Cambridge University Press.

Nuti, D.M. (1997b) Employee Ownership in Polish Privatizations. In: M. Uvalic and D.Vaughan-Whitehead, (eds), *Privatization Surprises in Transition Economies: employee-ownership in Central and Eastern Europe.* Cheltenham: Edward Elgar.

Nuti, D.M. (1998) Stocks and Stakes: The Case for Protecting Stakeholders Interests. *Economic Analysis*, **1**(1), 7-16.

Roland, G. and K. Sekkat (2000) Managerial Career Concerns, Privatization and Restructuring in Transition Economies. *European Economic Review*, **44**(10), 1857-72.

Schröder, P.J.H. (2001) On the Speed and Boundaries of Structural Adjustment when Fiscal Policy is Tight. *Economic Systems*, **25**(4), 345-364.

Schröder, P.J.H. (2003) Insider Privatization and Restructuring Incentives. *Economics of Planning*, **36**(4), 333-49.

Shleifer, A. and R.W. Vishny (1994) Politicians and Firms. *Quarterly Journal of Economics*, **109**, 995-1025.

Wright, P. and A. Mukherji (1999) Inside the Firm: Socioeconomic Versus Agency Perspectives on Firm Competitiveness. *Journal of Socio-Economics*, **28**, 295-307.

Chapter 3

Privatization, Efficiency, and Economic Growth[1]

Thorvaldur Gylfason

Privatization is shown to increase national economic output in a two-sector full-employment general-equilibrium model by enhancing efficiency as if a relative price distortion were being removed through price reform, trade liberalization, or stabilization. The static output gain from reallocation and reorganization through privatization is captured in a simple formula in which the gain is a quadratic function of the original distortion stemming from an excessive public sector. Substitution of plausible parameter values into the formula indicates that, in practice, the static output gain from privatization may be large. The potential dynamic output gain from privatization also appears to be substantial.

3.1 Introduction

Without exception, the economic and institutional reforms - liberalization, stabilization, and privatization - in the formerly planned economies of Central and Eastern Europe since 1989 have been accompanied by a substantial decrease in registered output, and then recovery. Inflation, previously suppressed through price controls, rose to high double-digit annual rates in Central and Eastern Europe and to triple-digit or even quadruple-digit rates in parts of the former Soviet Union, and then receded. Unemployment, concealed before, has become visible, and has jumped to double-digit rates in several countries in the region, while in others it has remained low - thanks, in part, to flexible labour markets.

---

[1] This study was initially prepared for an international conference on *Transition to Advanced Market Institutions and Economies* organized by the Systems Research Institute, Polish Academy of Sciences, and Polish Operational and Systems Research Society, Warsaw, 18-21 June 1997. Gylfi Magnusson, Gylfi Zoega, and two anonyous referees made helpful comments on earlier versions of the paper. Support from the Swedish Council for Humanistic and Social Science Research (HSFR) is gratefully acknowledged.

The effects of liberalization and stabilization on the path of output from plan to market have been analysed earlier, see, for example, Blanchard (1997), Bruno (1992), Borensztein, Demekas and Ostry (1993), Calvo and Coricelli (1993), and Williamson (1993). Here the aim is to offer a parallel analysis of the relationship between privatization and output and to show that all three, that is, liberalization, stabilization, and privatization, can be fitted into the same two-sector, general-equilibrium framework. To see the connection, consider first the effects of price and trade liberalization in a planned economy characterized initially by the full employment of all available resources and by excess aggregate demand, suppressed inflation, and a general shortage of goods and services (Gylfason, 1993). All factors of production are fixed. When prices are set free, the general price level rises. This general price increase is accompanied by a change in relative prices, because prices tend to increase most in those sectors, where the initial excess demand was strongest. At first, output falls and unemployment emerges as inefficient firms go bankrupt in those parts of the economy where the relative prices have fallen. The resulting contraction of aggregate supply increases the pressure on the price level. The slump in aggregate demand may also temporarily reduce output and employment in those markets where relative prices have risen, due to the spill-over effects of bankruptcies across sectors. This process continues until innovative entrepreneurs begin to exploit the new profit opportunities and incentives arising in markets where relative prices have risen. When this occurs, resources are drawn into more productive employment than before and the decline of total output is gradually reversed. The speed at which idle resources are thus absorbed into gainful employment elsewhere depends on many factors, including the local infrastructure and institutions, and the costs of adjustment and installation of new productive capacity (Mussa, 1982). Output keeps rising until all profit opportunities have been fully exploited and full employment has been restored at a higher level of output. By definition, more output from given inputs entails greater efficiency and thereby more rapid economic growth over time. This helps explain why the liberalization of domestic prices and foreign trade has tended to produce a sickle-shaped path of output in the transition from plan to market, essentially because it takes less time to destroy than to build: unprofitable enterprises can be closed down overnight, but the founding of new firms to take their place takes time (Figure 3.1).

This pattern is reinforced by the need to stabilize prices following the outbreak of inflation in the wake of liberalization (Gylfason, 1998). To see why, suppose that two types of capital, real and financial, both at constant prices, are used as inputs into production. Financial capital, including money, enables firms to economize on the use of other inputs (Fischer, 1974). To begin with, both types of capital are inefficiently employed, because suppressed inflation drives a wedge between the marginal returns to real and financial capital, and thus distorts efficiency. The restructuring and stabilization of the economy occur in two phases. Inflation rises at first and then recedes. In the initial, inflationary phase, some financial capital is replaced by physical capital in production. Because physical capital takes time to build and install, output contracts at first as financial capital is removed from production (e.g., tractors are idle, because the cash needed to keep them in running order is lacking), but this decline in output is tempered by the gradual accumulation of physical capital. Sooner or later, however, the second phase sets in as inflation is brought under control and money, credit, and other financial assets are drawn back into production. Profit-seeking entrepreneurs begin to exploit the business opportunities created by stable prices in an increasingly favorable business climate. As production begins to recover, inflation begins to slow down, and increased price stability will reinforce the expansion of output by improving the allocation and utilization of capital, thereby increasing economic efficiency.

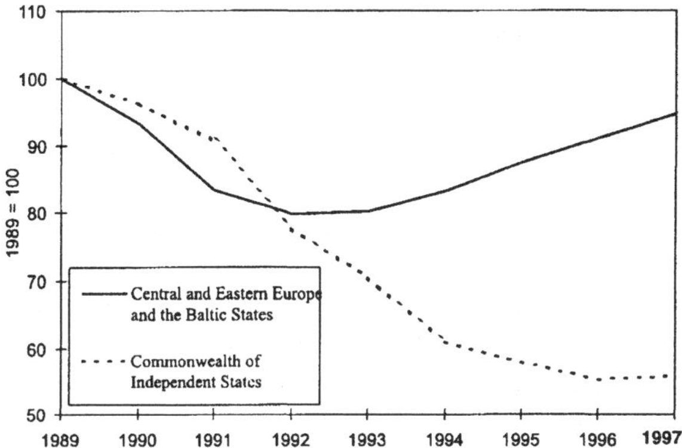

Figure 3.1 Central and Eastern Europe and the former Soviet Union: the path of output 1989-1997
Note: 1996 estimate and 1997 projection.
Source: European Bank for Reconstruction and Development, Transition Report 1997, Table 7.1.

As financial capital begins to grease the wheels of exchange and trade, total output rises little by little to a level corresponding to maximum efficiency in the allocation and utilization of real and financial capital and other resources. Thus, liberalization and stabilization produce a qualitatively similar sickle-shaped path of total output over time.

This chapter attempts to extend the above story to consider the reaction of output to privatization. By privatization is meant the transfer of productive capacity (as opposed to the provision of public goods) from the public sector to the private sector. By assumption, the public sector produces goods and services of lower quality, and at lower prices, than the private sector (Blanchard, 1997). This assumption seems to accord well with the experience of most communist countries. By driving a quality and price wedge between private and public output, an excessive public sector distorts production, and reduces its overall quality. The elimination of this distortion increases both the level of national economic output and its rate of growth over time.

Specifically, the aim of the chapter is:

(a) to show how the intersectoral reallocation of resources resulting from privatization ultimately increases total output at full employment by increasing economic efficiency as if a relative price distortion were being removed through either liberalization or stabilization, even though output may fall in the short run;
(b) to develop a simple formula in which the potential static output gain from reallocation through privatization is proportional to the square of the original quality and price distortion that has channeled too much of the country's productive resources into the public sector;
(c) to extend the formula by adding the output gain from reorganization (*viz.*, increased X-efficiency) to the output gain from intersectoral reallocation following privatization;
(d) to consider also the potential dynamic output gain, or growth bonus, from privatization when economic growth is endogenous in the presence of constant returns to capital in a broad sense; and
(e) to provide a rough quantitative assessment of the potential static and dynamic output gains from privatization by numerical simulations of conceivable scenarios.

The analysis to follow is not confined to the path of output from plan to market in Central and Eastern Europe and the former Soviet Union, where privatization has been only one of several factors (including, not least, the legacy from the past) influencing the behaviour of output during the transition period. On the contrary, the analysis is intended to be generally applicable and thus also applicable to the relationship between the size of the state-enterprise sector and economic growth in other parts of the world.

The main point of the chapter is that privatization, by reducing or removing harmful distortions caused by excessive subsidies and taxes and by thus increasing the overall quality and quantity of output, can play an important role in encouraging the reallocation of resources and the reorganization of production that are necessary to foster a favourable development of output and employment after the initial post-reform slump. In particular, privatization helps to raise not only the level of output per head, but also its rate of growth over time. In this respect, the quality and price distortion resulting from an oversized public sector is no different from the distortions that result from price controls or trade restrictions or from high inflation. The same general framework can be applied to all three phenomena – liberalization, stabilization, and privatization. This is the main message of the chapter.

3.2 Privatization and output: the static story

Output Y is produced in two ways, in the private sector (Y_{priv}) and in the public sector (Y_{pub}). Private and public output are one and the same good, but they differ in quality (see Blanchard, 1997). Private output is superior to and, therefore, commands a higher price than public output:

$$P_{priv} = (1+q)P_{pub} \tag{3.1}$$

where $q \geq 0$ represents the quality and price differential. This may stem, for example, from subsidies (at rate s) to public production and taxes (at rate t) on private production, so that, for consumers and producers to be willing to buy and sell both private and public output, we must have

$$(1-t)P_{priv} = (1+s)P_{pub}\,. \tag{3.2}$$

Equations (3.1) and (3.2) imply that

$$1+q = \frac{1+s}{1-t} \tag{3.3}$$

where q is simply a composite measure of the subsidies to public production and taxes on private production, which tend to direct resources from the private sector to the public sector, thereby reducing the overall quality of output. Privatization involves a reduction in the quality and price differential q, through lower subsidies to public production or less taxes on private production or both. By full privatization is meant the transfer of (almost) all state enterprises to the private sector; this brings q down to zero by reducing both s and t to zero. The production frontier is quadratic:

$$Y_{pub} = a - \frac{1}{2b} Y_{priv}^2 \tag{3.4}$$

where a and b are positive parameters. The frontier is described by the curve CEFD in Figure 3.2, where OC= a and OD= $\sqrt{2ba}$. Later on, an increase in private sector productivity will be represented by an increase in b, which moves the intercept D of the production frontier and the horizontal axis to the right.

Total net output (that is, national income) at constant prices, Y', is the sum of private and public output adjusted for taxes and subsidies:

$$Y' = (1-t)Y_{priv} + (1+s)Y_{pub}. \tag{3.5}$$

A balanced budget would require subsidies to be financed by taxes, so that $sY_{pub} = tY_{priv}$, in which case $Y' = Y_{priv} + Y_{pub}$.

If total output is expressed in terms of public output, with $Y = Y'/(1+s)$, then it follows from equation (3.5) that

$$Y = \left(\frac{1}{1+q}\right) Y_{priv} + Y_{pub} \tag{3.6}$$

where $1/(1+q)$ represents the net (after tax and subsidy) price ratio between private and public output. Equation (3.6) depicts the price line tangential to the production frontier at point E in Figure 3.2.

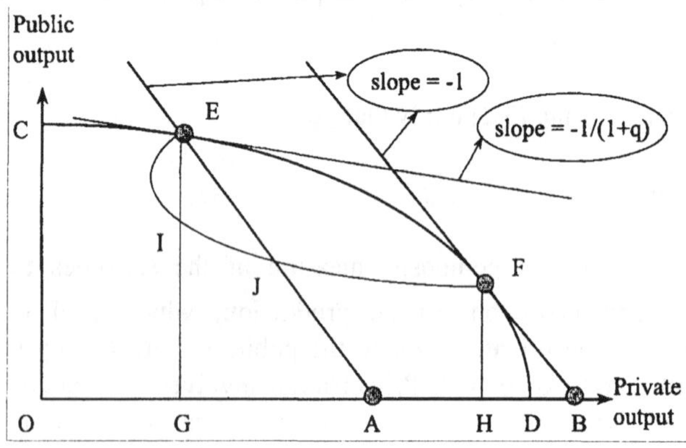

Figure 3.2 Reallocation gains from privatization

Figure 3.2 describes the optimal allocation of all available labour and capital between the two sectors. At point E in the figure, the marginal rate of transformation equals the net price ratio:

$$\frac{dY_{pub}}{dY_{priv}} = -\left(\frac{1}{b}\right)Y_{priv} = -\frac{1}{1+q} \tag{3.7}$$

so that, at E, we have

$$Y_{priv} = \frac{b}{1+q}. \tag{3.8}$$

This amount of Y_{priv} is shown by the distance OG in Figure 3.2. Hence, a decrease in subsidies or taxes, and thereby also in the quality and price differential q, increases private production. 'Full' privatization makes $q = 0$, bringing the economy from E to F, where $Y_{priv} = b$. This amount of Y_{priv} is shown as OH in Figure 3.2.

The change in Y_{priv} from E to F following full privatization (the distance GH in Figure 3.2) is therefore

$$\Delta Y_{priv} = b - \frac{b}{1+q} = \frac{bq}{1+q}. \tag{3.9}$$

The proportional increase in private output is simply

$$\frac{\Delta Y_{priv}}{Y_{priv}} = q. \tag{3.10}$$

Thus, the greater the initial quality and price differential between private and public output, the greater is the proportional increase in private production necessary to eradicate the differential through privatization.

The corresponding decrease in public output following privatization is found by a second-order Taylor expansion around point F in Figure 3.2:

$$\Delta Y_{pub} = f'(\Delta Y_{priv}) - \frac{1}{2}f''(\Delta Y_{priv})^2 = -\left(\frac{1}{b}\right)b\left(\frac{bq}{1+q}\right) - \frac{1}{2}\left(-\frac{1}{b}\right)\left(\frac{bq}{1+q}\right)^2 \tag{3.11}$$

where f is the quadratic function (3.4) and f' and f'' are its first and second derivatives.

By adding equations (3.9) and (3.11), the change in total output resulting from privatization can be shown to equal

$$\Delta Y = \frac{b}{2}\left(\frac{q}{1+q}\right)^2 . \tag{12}$$

The direct, static output gain from privatization at full employment is thus proportional to the square of the initial quality and price distortion.

Equation (3.12) can also be derived as follows. Before privatization, when the economy is in equilibrium at point E in Figure 3.2, total output can be measured in units of private output by the distance $\text{OA} = \text{OG} + \text{GA} = \text{OG} + \text{GE}$, because the slope of the line EA is -1. This gives

$$Y_E = \frac{b}{1+q} + a - \frac{1}{2b}\left(\frac{b}{1+q}\right)^2 . \tag{3.13}$$

After full privatization, when the economy reached equilibrium at point F, where q dropped to zero, total output is $\text{OB} = \text{OH} + \text{HB} = \text{OH} + \text{HF}$. This gives

$$Y_F = b + a - \frac{1}{2b}b^2 . \tag{3.14}$$

Subtracting equation (3.13) from equation (3.14) and simplifying we again get equation (3.12). The increase in total output from E to F is the distance AB.

At the margin, at point E, the effect on total output of an increase in q can be found by differentiating Y^E with respect to q in equation (3.13):

$$\frac{dY}{dq} = -\frac{bq}{(1+q)^3} < 0 . \tag{3.15}$$

Therefore, the elasticity of Y with respect to q, evaluated at the initial values of Y and Y_{priv}, is

$$\frac{dY}{dq}\frac{q}{Y} = -\frac{bq^2}{(1+q)^3 Y} = -\left(\frac{Y_{priv}}{Y}\right)\left(\frac{q}{1+q}\right)^2 . \tag{3.16}$$

The initial share of public output in total output can be found from equations (3.4), (3.6), and (3.8):

$$\frac{Y_{pub}}{Y} = \frac{2a(1+q)^2 - b}{2a(1+q)^2 + b} \leq 1. \tag{3.17}$$

The share of the public sector varies directly with q and tends to 1 as q tends to infinity, but it does not vanish when $q = 0$, as long as $a > b/2$.

By dividing through equation (3.12) by total post-privatization output Y, we can express the proportional rate of change of total output from E to F in Figure 3.2 as follows:

$$\frac{g}{1+g} = \frac{1}{2}\left(\frac{Y_{priv}}{Y}\right)\left(\frac{q}{1+q}\right)^2 \tag{18}$$

where g is the proportional change in output (with initial output as a base, i.e., AB/OA in the figure) and Y_{priv}/Y is the pre-privatization share of the private sector in total output; see equation (3.17). The change in output varies directly with (i) the scale of the privatization (the larger the chunk of public production that is transferred to the private sector, the greater will be the resulting increase in output) and (ii) the magnitude of the initial quality and price distortion q (the greater the distortion, the greater will be the gain from removing it).

3.2.1 Reallocation versus reorganization

The efficiency gains discussed thus far arise solely from the reallocation of resources from the public sector to the private sector. There is reason to expect, however, that privatization also encourages reorganization within the private sector, and thus increases its productivity in addition to the gains from intersectoral reallocation. To deal with this possibility, let us now extend the model by assuming that private-sector productivity increases in proportion to the initial quality and price differential, according to

$$\frac{\Delta b}{b} = kq \tag{3.19}$$

where k is a positive constant (for another way of introducing increased X-efficiency into a static model of intersectoral resource allocation, see Gylfason, 1995). When productivity growth is added to the model, the production frontier moves to the right from OCD to OCM as shown in Figure 3.3. A new equilibrium is reached at point K. The reallocation gain is shown as before by the distance AB in Figure 3.2, and the reorganization gain is shown as BQ in Figure 3.3.

Let us now develop the expression for the latter gain, from reorganization.

The production frontier in equation (3.4) needs to be changed to

$$Y_{pub} = a - \frac{1}{2b(1+kq)} Y_{priv}^2 \tag{3.20}$$

to reflect the outward shift shown in Figure 3.3, where $OM = \sqrt{2ab(1+kq)}$, and $OD = \sqrt{2ba}$ and $OC = a$ as before. In view of equation (3.19), the coefficient b in equation (3.4) has been replaced by $b(1+kq)$ in equation (20) to reflect the assumed increase in private-sector productivity.

We proceed in two steps. First, let us find the increase in private output.

At point K in the Figure 3.3, where $dY_{pub}/dY_{priv} = -1$, we see from equation (3.20) that $Y_{priv} = b(1+kq)$. Comparing this with $Y_{priv} = b$ at point F, we see that the increase in private output from F to K is

$$\Delta Y_{priv} = b(1+kq) - b = bkq\ . \tag{3.21}$$

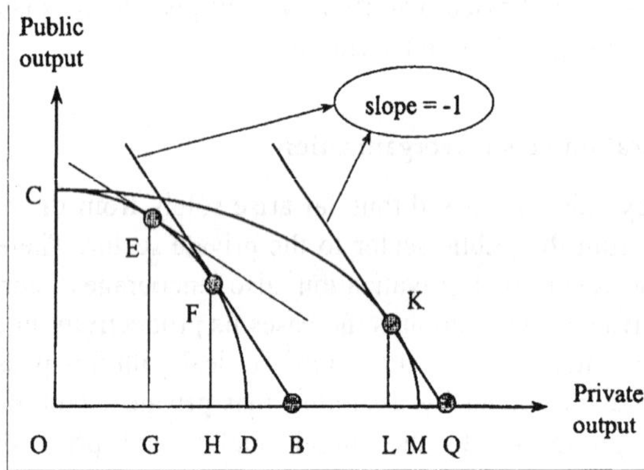

Figure 3.3 Reorganization gains from privatization

This increase is shown by the distance HL in Figure 3.3. The proportional increase in Y_{priv} is kq.

The corresponding decrease in public output is found by plugging these equilibrium values of Y_{priv} at F and K in Figure 3.3 back into equation (3.20). Geometrically, we see from the figure that the additional decrease in Y_{pub} amounts to HF-LK in the figure, which is equal to HB-LQ, because the slope of the lines FB and KQ is -1. We find HF by substituting $Y_{priv} = b$ at F into equation (3.4) to get $Y_{pub} = a - b/2$. Therefore, at post-reform prices (with $q = 0$), $Y = Y_{priv} + Y_{pub} = a + b/2$, as in equation (3.14). To find LK, we substitute $Y_{priv} = b(1 + kq)$ at K into equation (3.20) to find $Y_{pub} = a - b(1 + kq)/2$. Adding Y_{priv} and Y_{pub} at K, we obtain

$$Y_K = a + \frac{b(1 + kq)}{2}. \tag{3.22}$$

The change in public output from F to K is given by

$$\Delta Y_{pub} = \left(a - \frac{b(1 + kq)}{2}\right) - \left(a - \frac{b}{2}\right) = -\frac{bkq}{2}. \tag{3.23}$$

Adding equations (3.21) and (3.23) shows that total output has increased by $bkq - bkq/2 = bkq/2$. Equivalently, the increase in output from F to K can be measured directly as

$$\Delta Y = \left(a + \frac{b(1 + kq)}{2}\right) - \left(a + \frac{b}{2}\right) = \frac{bkq}{2}. \tag{3.24}$$

This expression represents the gain from reorganization. Adding this to the gain from reallocation shown in equation (3.12), we get the following result for the total output gain from privatization:

$$\Delta Y = \frac{b}{2}\left[\left(\frac{q}{1 + q}\right)^2 + kq\right]. \tag{3.25}$$

Equation (3.25) simplifies to equation (3.12) when the gains from reorganization are left out ($k = 0$).

Equations (3.8), (3.9), and (3.21) imply that the proportional increase in private output from E to K is

$$\frac{\Delta Y_{priv}}{Y_{priv}} = \frac{bq\left(\frac{1}{1 + q}\right) + k}{\frac{b}{1 + q}} = q[1 + k(1 + q)]. \tag{3.26}$$

Thus, the greater (i) the initial quality and price differential between private and public output and (ii) the stimulus to productivity in the private sector, the greater is the proportional increase in private production necessary to eradicate the distortion through privatization.

Equation (3.26) simplifies to equation (3.10) when productivity does not respond to privatization ($k = 0$).

The share of public sector output in total output at the final equilibrium point K in Figure 3.3 is

$$\frac{Y_{pub}}{Y} = \frac{2a - b(1 + kq)}{2a + b(1 + kq)} \leq 1 . \tag{3.27}$$

The corresponding share of private output in total output at K is

$$\frac{Y_{priv}}{Y} = \frac{2b(1 + kq)}{2a + b(1 + kq)} . \tag{3.28}$$

The sum of the two shares in equations (3.27) and (3.28) is 1.

At last, the proportional increase in total output from E to K is found by dividing through equation (3.25) by total output at K and using equation (3.28):

$$\frac{g}{1+g} = \frac{1}{2}\left(\frac{Y_{priv}}{Y}\right)\left[\left(\frac{q}{1+q}\right)^2 + kq\right]\left(\frac{1}{1+kq}\right) . \tag{3.29}$$

The ultimate output gain from privatization, from E to F in Figure 3.2 or from E to K in Figure 3.3, may be preceded by an economic downturn and increased unemployment. Privatization involves the restructuring or closure of bankrupt enterprises, and the reallocation of labour and capital released in the process to new firms in other industries or locations may take time.

In particular, the decrease in incomes in the public sector may reduce purchases from the private sector, so that both sectors decline in the early stages of reform. Therefore, output may follow a path such as EIJF in Figure 3.2. At I, private output is restored to its pre-reform level, and at J, national income is restored to its pre-reform level, before it settles at F.

3.2.2 Numerical examples

The model outlined above enables us to quantify the output gains from privatization. For example, equation (3.18) enables us to assess the output gain from reallocation on the basis of just two parameters: (i) the post-reform share of the private sector in total output Y_{priv}/Y from equation (3.17), and (ii) the pre-reform quality and price differential from equations (3.1) to (3.3). If, for instance, the share of the private sector in total output is increased to 8/9 and if $q=1$, then $g=0.125$ by equation (3.18).

Consider now a somewhat more elaborate numerical example to get a better feel of the model. Set $s=0.5$ and $t=0.25$; this makes $q=1$ as before.

Further, set $a=125$ and $b=200$ in equation (3.4). Then, initially, $Y_{priv}^{E}=100$ by equation (3.8) and $Y_{pub}^{E}=100$ by equation (3.4). That makes total output at the initial equilibrium point E in Figures 3.2 and 3.3 equal to $Y^{E}=100+100=200$, assessed at the post-reform price ratio (which is 1 when $q=0$). Suppose, to start with, that $k=0$. Privatization then increases Y_{priv} by 100 conform to equation (3.9) and decreases Y_{pub} by 75 conform to equation (3.11), so that total output Y increases by 25 (=100-75), or by 12.5 per cent, from E to F in the figures. This is consistent with $Y_E=200$ and $Y_F=225$ from equations (3.13) and (3.14). The share of the private sector in total output has increased to 8/9 (=200/225), as confirmed by equation (3.17) when $q=0$. Substituting this value of Y_{priv}/Y into equation (3.18) further confirms that total output has increased by 12.5 per cent. This is the reallocation effect of privatization.

Now consider also the reorganization effect and set $k=0.2$. Privatization now increases Y_{priv} by 100 from E to F as before and further by 40 by equation (3.21) and becomes 240 (=100+100+40), which is an increase by 140 per cent *in toto*, see equation (3.26). As before, Y_{pub} decreases by 75 from E to F by equation (3.11) and further by 20 by equation (3.23) and becomes 5 (=100-75-20). Total output Y increases as a result by 45 (=140-95), or by 22.5 per cent, as is confirmed by comparing $Y_K=245$ from equation (3.22) with $Y_E=200$ from equation (3.13). The same result obtains by computing $g=0.225$ from equation (3.29), using the result that privatization reduces the share of the public sector in total output from 2/3 to 1/49 by equations (3.17) and (3.27).

Thus, full privatization, resulting in $q=0$, does not lead to the eradication of public production in this case.

In order to get a fuller picture of the possible macroeconomic and empirical significance of increased efficiency in the allocation of resources through privatization, let us now experiment with plausible parameter values in equation (3.29). This is clearly a highly speculative exercise because of the simplicity of the formula and the unavailability of reliable evidence about the explanatory parameters.

Let us assume the price of public output initially to be out of line with the price of private output by a factor of 2, 3, 4, or 5, so that q takes the values 1, 2, 3, and 4; see equation (3.1). Further, assume the share of the private sector in total output following privatization to range from 0.5 to 0.9. For comparison, the average share of state-owned enterprises in economic activity in 8 industrial countries and 40 developing countries in 1988 was 6 per cent and 11 per cent, respectively (see World Bank, 1995). At last, set k equal to 0 in Panel A and 0.2 in Panel B. The proportional output gains that follow from these assumptions are shown in Table 3.1.

Table 3.1 Static output gains from privatization

Panel A. Gains from reallocation			
k=0	$Y_{priv}/Y=0.5$	$Y_{priv}/Y=0.7$	$Y_{priv}/Y=0.9$
q=1	g=0.07	g=0.10	g=0.13
q=2	g=0.13	g=0.19	g=0.25
q=3	g=0.16	g=0.25	g=0.34
q=4	g=0.19	g=0.29	g=0.40
Panel B. Gains from reallocation and reorganization			
k=0.2	$Y_{priv}/Y=0.5$	$Y_{priv}/Y=0.7$	$Y_{priv}/Y=0.9$
q=1	g=0.10	g=0.15	g=0.20
q=2	g=0.18	g=0.27	g=0.37
q=3	g=0.22	g=0.34	g=0.49
q=4	g=0.25	g=0.39	g=0.56

Source: Author's computations based on equation (3.29)

Subject to the underlying assumptions made about the parameters of the model, the numbers in Table 3.1 imply that the proportional static output gains from privatization can range from 7 per cent to 56 per cent once and for all. These gains are permanent, *ceteris paribus*. A greater reaction of private sector productivity to privatization would result in still higher numbers in Panel B.

Given a discount rate of 5 per cent per year, the present value of these gains amounts to 1.4 to 11.2 times annual national income once and for all.

For comparison, the smallest figure in the table ($g = 0.07$) exceeds the rough estimates of the permanent static output gains expected to emerge gradually from the market unification of Europe in 1992 according to Cecchini (1988).

If these numbers are at all indicative of the results that would emerge from detailed empirical case studies, it seems reasonable to conclude that failing to privatize may be expensive indeed, provided that the initial slump in output is not too deep and does not last too long.

3.3 From efficiency to growth

How do the static output gains from privatization reported in the previous section influence economic growth over time?

According to the neoclassical growth model, the effects of increased static efficiency on growth can only be temporary. They may be large and they may last long, even for decades, but eventually they will peter out, because growth is ultimately an exogenous variable in the neoclassical model.

Here, instead, we adopt the simplest possible learning-by-doing version of the theory of endogenous growth (see, for instance, Romer, 1986, 1989). Suppose output is produced by labour L and capital K through a Cobb-Douglas production function:

$$Y = AL^{a}K^{1-a} . \tag{3.30}$$

Let the accumulated technological know-how represented by A be tied to the capital/labor ratio by

$$A = E\left(\frac{K}{L}\right)^{a} \tag{3.31}$$

where E is a constant. This is what is meant by learning-by-doing: by using capital, workers learn how to use it more efficiently. It follows that

$$Y = EK \tag{3.32}$$

where E reflects efficiency. Output Y depends solely on the capital stock K and the efficiency E with which it is used in production. Output depends, in other words, on the quantity and quality of capital. Because E is a constant, output and capital must grow at the same rate, g.

Suppose now that saving S is proportional to output and equals gross investment, that is, $I = \Delta K + \delta K$, where δ is the depreciation rate. Then

$$S = sY = I = \Delta K + \delta K = \frac{\Delta Y}{E} + \frac{\delta Y}{E} \tag{3.33}$$

for given E, so that

$$g = sE - \delta . \tag{3.34}$$

The rate of economic growth, in words, equals the multiple of the saving rate and the efficiency of capital use E less the depreciation rate δ. This is simply a restatement of the Harrod-Domar model of growth, with the addition, due to Romer (1986), that output growth here is not constrained by population growth, see also Grossman and Helpman (1991).

Profit maximization requires that the marginal product of capital be equal to the gross rate of interest, $r + \delta$:

$$\frac{dY}{dK} = (1-a)\frac{Y}{K} = (1-a)E = r + \delta . \tag{3.35}$$

In a closed economy, r can be viewed as an endogenous variable and E as an exogenous variable: $r = (1-a)E - \delta$ by equation (3.35). If, for example, the capital share $1-a = 1/3$, $E = 0.3$, and $\delta = 0.06$, then $r = 0.04$. If the Golden Rule holds, then $s = 1-a$ and, hence, $g = r$ by equations (3.34) and (3.35). Therefore, an exogenous increase in E - for example, through privatization - will raise both r and g. In a small open economy, the roles of E and r are reversed: r, the domestic interest rate, then mirrors the foreign interest rate, which is exogenous from the home country's point of view and E becomes endogenous.

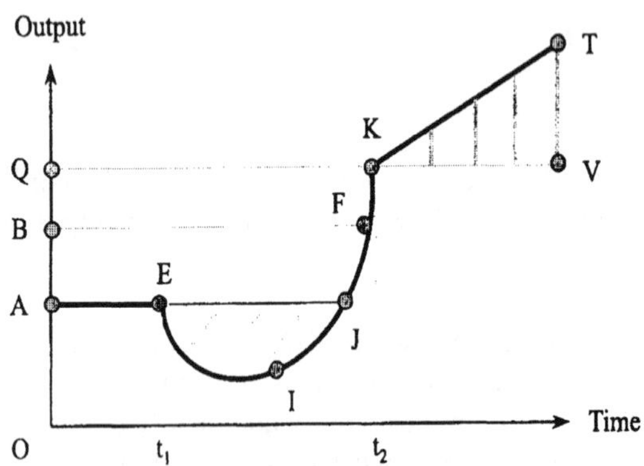

Figure 3.4 The path of output following privatization

Generally, E reflects the efficiency of resource allocation and organization in the economy. Therefore, all improvements in efficiency - due, for instance, to privatization, price reform, trade liberalization, and education - result not only in a permanently higher level of output by equation (3.25), but also a permanently higher rate of growth of output by equation (3.34), see Easterly (1992) for a model of the linkages between production distortions and endogenous growth. Therefore, the economy follows the sickle-shaped path EIJFKT rather than EIJFKV in Figure 3.4, where the labelling of the vertical axis conforms to Figures 3.2 and 3.3. The area KTV represents the dynamic output gain from economic reform.

How large is this potential growth bonus? Consider, as an example, an economy where saving is 20 per cent of output ($s = 0.2$), depreciation is 6 per cent of the capital stock ($\delta = 0.06$), and the efficiency parameter E is 0.3 initially, which implies a capital/output ratio of 3.3. Then, by equation (3.34), the growth rate g is zero as shown in Table 3.2. If the efficiency of capital use increases by 20 per cent in the sense that output rises by that much for a given capital stock, see Table 3.1, then E becomes 0.36 and the rate of growth rises from zero to 1.2 per cent per year. This increase in growth is permanent by the construction of the production function (3.32).

Specifically, the mechanisms that prevent more efficiency and more saving from stimulating growth permanently in the Harrod-Domar model and in the neoclassical model are absent here, because the production function (3.32) exhibits constant returns to capital. In the neoclassical model, increased static efficiency through privatization is equivalent to a technological innovation that raises the rate of growth of output only as long as it takes the economy to move from one steady-state growth path to another, higher path. However, this adjustment process may take a long time. The medium-term properties of the neoclassical model may, therefore, be difficult to distinguish empirically from the long-run properties of the endogenous-growth model employed here.

Table 3.2 Dynamic output gains from privatization

δ =0.06	**E=0.30**	**E=0.36**	**E=0.45**
s=0.10	g=-0.03	g=-0.024	g=-0.015
s=0.20	g=0	g=0.012	g=0.03
s=0.30	g=0.03	g=0.048	g=0.075
s=0.40	g=0.06	g=0.084	g=0.12

Source: Author's computations based on equation (3.34)

At an annual rate of growth of 3 per cent, output per head will double every 24 years, *ceteris paribus*. Given $E = 0.3$, each 10 point increase in the saving rate would increase growth by 3 percentage points. A simultaneous 10 point increase in the saving rate (say, from 0.20 to 0.30) and a 20 per cent increase in efficiency would raise the growth rate from nothing to 4.8 per cent per year, and would double output per head in less than 15 years, and so on.

What if there is no learning-by-doing? Then we are back in the neoclassical world, where economic growth is exogenous. If the production function is rewritten in per capita terms: $y = Ak^{1-a}$, where $y = Y/L$ and $k = K/L$, then equation (3.35) becomes $dy/dk = (1-a)Ak^{-a} = r + \delta$. Solving this equation for *k*, substituting the result into the production function, and applying the Golden Rule, we obtain the following approximation to per capita output:

$$y = A^{\frac{1}{a}} s^{\frac{1-a}{a}} (r+\delta)^{-\left(\frac{1-a}{a}\right)} \qquad (3.36)$$

whereby the long-run steady-state level of *per capita* output varies directly with technology (that is, efficiency) and the saving rate, and inversely with the rates of interest and depreciation. In this case, if there is no dynamic growth in *A*, meaning that privatization produces only static gains in efficiency, as in Section 2, there will be no growth in *y* either (*Y* grows at the same rate as *L*, the population).

Note that the approximation involved in (3.36) is harmless. An exact formulation requires replacing the exponents 1/*a* and (1-*a*)/*a* in equation (3.36) by 1/(1-*s*) and *s*/(1-*s*) in full compliance with the Golden Rule. The Golden Rule is equivalent to the Ramsey Rule when the intertemporal elasticity of substitution is 1 and the discount rate is 0.

Even so, static efficiency gains can exert a strong influence on steady-state *per capita* output in the long run. Suppose, for instance, that *a*=2/3. Then, by equation (3.36), a 20 per cent increase in efficiency will raise per capita output by 30 per cent, and a 50 per cent increase in A will raise *y* by 75 per cent, *ceteris paribus*.

Observed differences in per capita output across countries do not seem to exceed the possibilities suggested by equation (3.36). If we set $r = 0$ for simplicity and $a = 2/3$ as above, the ratio of a rich country's per capita, y_R, to that of a poor country, y_P, is approximately

$$\frac{y_R}{y_P} = \left(\frac{A_R}{A_P}\right)^{\frac{3}{2}} \left(\frac{s_R}{s_P}\right)^{\frac{1}{2}} \left(\frac{\delta_R}{\delta_P}\right)^{\frac{1}{2}}. \qquad (3.37)$$

Thus, if the rich country saves twice as much as the poor country and depreciates its capital stock at only half the latter's pace (because of the former's more profitable investment in the past), then a tenfold difference in income means a threefold difference in efficiency. For the same assumptions about s and δ, an income ratio of $y_R/y_p = 20$ implies $A_R/A_p = 4.7$. The result is about the same if the exponents in equation (3.37) are changed in accordance with the Golden Rule, as mentioned before. The result is also about the same if the interest rate is set equal to, say, 4 per cent rather than 0.

To take a concrete case, consider Korea and Uganda, whose purchasing-power-parity-adjusted per capita GNP in 1995 were, respectively, US 11,450 and US 1,470. Their saving (or rather investment) rates were 37 per cent and 16 per cent (see World Bank, 1997). Then, even if their depreciation rates were the same, the income ratio of 7.8 between the two countries implies an efficiency differential of 3.0. It seems safe to conclude that differences between efficiency, saving and investment rates, and depreciation across countries can go a long way towards explaining why their living standards - and, by implication, why their growth rates on their way to their steady states - differ.

3.4 Conclusion

In this chapter an attempt has been made to clarify the effects of privatization on the level of national income and its rate of growth over time. The static output gain from privatization was modelled as involving the elimination of a quality and price differential between private and public output. Within the framework of a two-sector full-employment general-equilibrium model, the efficiency gain from eliminating the quality and price distortion involved was captured in a simple formula in which the gain is related to the square of the original distortion. Substitution of plausible parameter values into the formula suggests that the total output gain from privatization may be substantial. Because of the efficiency boost that results from the intersectoral reallocation of resources and from reorganization, economic growth increases permanently according to the new theory of endogenous growth, or at least for a time according to the neoclassical growth model. The dynamic output gain is also likely to be large.

References

Blanchard, O. (1997) *The Economics of Post-Communist Transition*. Oxford: Clarendon Press.

Borensztein, E., D.G. Demekas, and J.D. Ostry (1993) An Empirical Analysis of the Output Declines in Three Eastern European Countries. *IMF Staff Papers*, **40**(1), March, 1-31.

Bruno, M. (1992) Stabilization and Reform in Eastern Europe. *IMF Staff Papers*, **39**(4), December, 741-77.

Calvo, G.A., and F. Coricelli (1993) Output Collapse in Eastern Europe. *IMF Staff Papers*, **40**(1), March, 32-52.

Cecchini, P. (1988) *The European Challenge 1992*. Aldershot: Gower.

Easterly, W. (1992) Endogenous Growth in Developing Countries with Government-induced Distortions. Chapter 9 in: V. Corbo, S. Fischer, and S.B. Webb (eds.) *Adjustment Lending Revisited*. Washington, DC: The World Bank.

Fischer, S. (1974) Money and the Production Function. *Economic Inquiry*, **12**, December, 517-33.

Grossman, G., and E. Helpman (1991) *Innovation and Growth in the Global Economy*. Cambridge, MA and London: MIT Press.

Gylfason, T. (1993) Output Gains from Economic Liberalization: A Simple Formula. Chapter 4 in L. Somogyi (ed.) *The Political Economy of the Transition Process in Eastern Europe*. London: Edward Elgar.

Gylfason, T. (1995) The Macroeconomics of European Agriculture. *Princeton Studies in International Finance*, **78**, May.

Gylfason, T. (1998) Output Gains from Economic Stabilization. *Journal of Development Economics*, **56**(1), 81-96.

Mussa, M. (1982) Government Policy and the Adjustment Process. In: J.N. Bhagwati (ed.) *Import Competition and Response*. Cambridge, MA: The University of Chicago Press and National Bureau of Economic Research, 73-120.

Romer, P.M. (1986) Increasing Returns and Long-run Growth. *Journal of Political Economy*, **94**, October, 1002-37.

Romer, P.M. (1989) Capital Accumulation in the Theory of Long Run Growth. In: R.J. Barro (ed.) *Modern Business Cycle Theory*. Cambridge, MA: Harvard University Press, 51-127.

Williamson, J. (1993) Why Did Output Fall in Eastern Europe? Chapter 2 in: L. Somogyi (ed.) *The Political Economy of the Transition Process in Eastern Europe*. London: Edward Elgar.

World Bank (1995) *Bureaucrats in Business: The Economics and Politics of Government Ownership*. Oxford: Oxford University Press.

World Bank (1997) *World Development Report*. Oxford: Oxford University Press.

Chapter 4

How the System Worked, or: The Herring Barrel Metaphor[1]

Jan W. Owsiński

A metaphor is presented, illustrating the mechanism of functioning of the communist system. The metaphor, which is called the herring barrel metaphor, and is developed on the basis of very few initial presuppositions, provides a very detailed image of the way the communist system worked, along with a number of characteristic and unique side-effects, like quasi-non-existent unemployment, low wages, shortages, etc. It can therefore be treated as a verbal model, which might in at least some of its aspects turned into a quantitative model. Most importantly, the model shows that shortage was the driving force and the basis of functioning of the system, the main consequence being that the shortage-based exchange power rather than income or any other status indicator decided of people's positions and capacities.

4.1 Introductory remarks

The quasi-totalitarian communist system implementations of Central Europe had their terrifying historical periods. They ended for the majority of the European communist countries around 1956, although some of the most inhuman features of the system dragged on well into the 1980s, surfacing from time to time in the form, for instance, of invasion of Czechoslovakia in 1968, the German-German border with automatically shooting 'security' facilities, the Rumanian bloodshed of 1989, or the martial law period in Poland.

Still, everyday life in these countries over at least the last two decades preceding the 1989 was not wholly characterized by fear, terror, hunger, or street violence. The predominant image of life in the communist countries of Europe was that it was dull, grey and low profile, but also

[1] The Herring Barrel Metaphor was published in its initial version as a paper in the journal *Control & Cybernetics* in 1992 under the title A metaphoric system of economy: the Herring Barrel Metaphor (Owsiński, 1992). The present paper extends significantly the explanations linking the metaphor with its real-world counterpart and the final part devoted to the post-change behaviour.

stable, predictable and slow (involving decreased levels of effort). That is how life was perceived here both from the outside and from the inside. It is true that thousands wanted to emigrate from here to Western Europe, North America and Australia, but almost none of those wishing to leave was threatened in the twenty years before 1989 with death, neither of hunger nor from the hands of some death squads.

Thus, people were fleeing closed quarters, lack of broader perspectives and eternal, it seemed, lines. They had in their minds the image of a richer, broader and freer world, in which there is more to consume, to reach for and, simply, to do. In fact, very few of them were running for their life.

At the same time the system has been propagating the image of both external and internal stability and expansion. Some feared it might play the role of modern Mongols or Barbarians, who would turn, on purpose, Western civilisation to ruins.

Although the system seems to be altogether disappearing, both this particular form of totalitarian rule and other similar forms are still and will continue to woo political and social groups of various countries. We have to be alert. On the other hand, we have to understand how the system worked in order to understand the difficulties of doing away with it.

This chapter presents a very simple metaphor for an economic and political system based upon the principles of shortage and distribution. This metaphor provides an effective measure for describing a certain class of economic, social and political phenomena well known from the experience of the "real socialist", or what was called in the West: "communist" countries. It presents a rationale for the working of the system in conditions of apparent equality, full employment, ineffectiveness, lack of true information, dual economy etc. The chapter goes on to show the most important difficulties of transition to an open economy and democratic society.

4.2 The system

1. Imagine a country, whose government, due to a war or a natural catastrophe, had to revert (for a finite period of time, of course) to special anti-speculation measures. Moreover, in order to avoid inflation, which might result from the scarcity of many important goods, market mechanisms were almost totally abandoned[2].

---

[2] In most instances communism, or real socialism, was actually introduced in conditions of severe economic difficulties (e.g. just after World War II, after or with the de-colonisation, etc.).

For a better insight into the consequences of such moves let us consider a small shop, selling herrings.

Each morning a van arrives at the shop, bringing a barrel of salted herring. The barrel is then normally put behind the counter. (This is important insofar as behind the counter no customer can see how many herrings are there still in the barrel.) In conditions of the - already commonly known - shortage there is every day a queue of people waiting for the herrings.

The herring seller is paid a flat salary, regardless of the volume of sales of herrings, over which, in any case, he has very little influence.

Queues, however, exist not only at the herring shop. The herring seller is fully aware of this. He himself is looking for several goods and services, for which queues are being formed every day. He is not sure whether he can get all of these, especially as he has his own work to do. But, on the other hand, he also knows that, from time to time, the sellers of these other goods and services line up for the herring. That is where his hope lies. As long as there is a queue, and as long as there is uncertainty as to whether everybody in the line shall have their demand satisfied, the herring seller may hope that will be able to exchange herrings at his disposal for these other goods and services.[3]

True, if everybody were sure of getting what they want, even at a cost of some queueing[4], there would be no motivation for such an exchange of goods and services among sellers (or, more properly distributors). But the uncertainty is there, so that the herring seller is performing his behind-the-counter trick in order to secure herrings for those of exchange value for him.

2. Thus, the herring seller owes his capacity of getting the needed goods and services to the uncertainty as to obtaining herrings in his shop. Therefore, he is interested in maintaining the expected proportion of the length of queue, which gets served from day to day at, say, 80 to 90 per cent, so as not to cause rebellion, on the one hand, and to retain his exchange power, on the other. Of course, his control over the situation in the herring shop is limited, but it is sufficient to absorb slow changes in supply and/or demand.

---

[3] The metaphor disregards, on purpose, the role of money and prices, which was often just symbolic (centralized price setting motivated primarily by political reasons), while the essential capacity of acquiring was associated with the exchange power. It also disregards the various scopes of functioning of the market, which existed in some of the communist countries, always strictly limited and controlled, and usually of special purpose political nature (like small trade and catering in the German Democratic Republic or private farming in Poland).

[4] Within certain limits, posed by the minimum time necessary for doing one's work (and/or pretending to do it) and for other activities.

So, even if one day there were plenty - or, say, enough - of all those searched for goods and services, the herring seller shall use all tricks available to him in order to get rid of the surplus and cut down the served proportion of the queue to the normal dimensions, i.e. 80-90 per cent of the line. This can be done, e.g. by giving a little more to his better clients and telling them this is a special opportunity before the price hike, or by simple dumping (the surplus has a negative value for him). On the other hand, in exactly the same way, the herring seller is unable to look behind the counters of his exchange partners, and so he shall never know for sure what goes on with the other goods and services, and his interest in the shortage of herring shall persist.

3. Hence, we have reached the first truth about such a system: *all those in power of distributing goods and services are positively interested in a certain (optimal) degree of shortage*. It is *from shortage* that *power is reaped*. And therefore power, not economy, and shortage, not wealth, are the motive force of the system. This, though, is not everything that is to the system.

4. By keeping the non-served proportion of the queue at a certain not-too-high level the herring seller is keeping away the threat of counteraction from the customers, since the probability that a customer not served on any one day may get served on another day (or when additional measures are undertaken) is sufficiently high. This, however, is usually not satisfactory. The customers are in fact asking why there are still not enough herrings, although the catastrophe (or war) that started the system occurred so long ago. On the other hand, the superiors of the herring seller may know that the supplies are on the increase, and may still hear of inadequacy of supplies. What, then? Then, the herring seller, the sole owner of his, albeit very narrow, truth, is resorting to another set of tricks, even though quite old and worn out ones. The first is: the speculators and those who amass reserves are buying too much. Such explanation is plausible in conditions of - known - shortage, cannot be easily verified and is quite satisfactory, as we shall see, for the herring seller's superiors. The other trick consists in waving his finger conspicuously in the direction of some of *them* (who have installed and still run the system, that is), which may effectively channel public discontent. The situation is similar for the other sellers/distributors.

5. The system is therefore characterized by the *inherent lack of true information*, not only concerning supply and demand - in fact, lack of truth in general. It is in the interest of all sellers to conceal the truth, and there is no mechanism to make it surface. Even if they suspect, and perhaps with time become certain, that the other distributors play the (same) shortage trick, while in reality there is enough of (at least some)

goods, they are neither interested in dismantling the system, in which they dispose of definite power, nor capable of doing this in the face of all those positively interested in power resulting from the distribution of shortage and concealment of information.[5]

On the top of this, the explanations given for the causes of the situation are false, by definition.

6. Now, at a certain time point the herring seller may, if the system is working properly, abandon completely his salary. Wow! Look! What a new era for humanity: not only are distributors not gaining more than humble you, but they are actively fighting for your well-being at, virtually, no cost to you.[6] True, the only risk (other than revolution) for the herring seller is that he may get fired, or that more herring shops will open, or that counters be transparent, so that eventually everybody gets served. In fact, only the first of these threats is real.

7. Since the positions of herring sellers are highly valued, people are also, although in a different way (it takes, first of all, knowing how to), lining up to get these positions. Now, everything that has been said of the line in the herring shop applies to this superior-level line as well. There is no market at this level, neither, and the position of the superior who assigns people to the herring-selling jobs is valued only when there is an adequately short supply of such positions, even though the ultimate demand for herring would require more herring shops. A person lining up for a herring seller's position may be a son of someone who distributes cars, wife of someone who might give you a construction plot ("down with land speculation and skyrocketing land prices!"), or brother of the

---

[5] Note that this is an essential dual characteristic of the communist system, observed in practice: the distribution paradigm enables the planning approach and the proposition that all demands and supplies can be appropriately balanced, also using corresponding mathematical models, and at the same time - all the information that is fed to the balancing system of calculations is false (e.g. labour productivity, lowered significantly by the necessity of standing in lines).

[6] This is why *all the comparisons of income distribution from before and after the post-communist transformation are fully unreliable: most of the actual income, for a large portion of the populations, did not have any monetary expression.* It was the exchange capacity and the goods (and services) that could thereby be obtained that mattered. A striking example is provided by the housing sector. There exiṣted several manners of acquiring an apartment, ranging from simple assignment at no cost (e.g. to the top level distributors) to simple market-like purchase. The closer one wanted to get to the former manner of acquisition, the bigger was the share of non-monetary contribution to the cost (e.g. getting appropriate certificates of need of an apartment, creating a secondary exchange market for such certificates).

toilet-paper plant director. In this way one is really able to get - almost - everything.

8. The setting repeats itself at consecutive levels up to the top and thereby a coherent system of shortage, distribution, concealed information, and personal power is formed, internally cognised and maintained.

9. The system has two ethical (and legal) sides: the external one, showing equality, stability, full employment, lack of "individualistic greed" and "animal-like competition" (along with the "temporary", even though ubiquitous, shortages), and the internal one, reserved to those in positions of power, where only subordination, strict execution of orders, exchange relations and maintenance of the system count.[7]

10. Because of the inherently dual character, the system is run through a dual institutional setting. The first component is a simile of the usual power system, with elections, social associations (e.g. trade unions, trade and interest societies, etc.), parliament, government and local administration. The second, the proper power-wielding organization, is also official, but its actual power and functioning is largely unofficial. It is this second systemic component that runs the distribution system, while the first one is held responsible for whatever is to be ultimately (end-of-the-line) distributed (e.g. how much herring there is). The first component is subordinated to the second one in terms of the essential aspects of the distribution system.[8]

11. Thus, the entire system is organized and run in a mob-like manner - no written orders, no traces[9], and double morality, where any member of the (big) family can be destroyed, if not by killing, then simply by exposing him to the official (external) justice, for the border between

[7] Note that even if the system has not started from the ideological precepts of communism, these precepts would have been invented on the way as the optimum justification for the distribution system in order to preserve the power of the distributors.

[8] The second component was usually constituted by the (communist) "Party", although in several real-socialist countries this was, at least officially, not the only party on the political scene. This was, in particular, the case of Poland and of the German Democratic Republic, where satellite parties could formally function, entirely subordinated to the Party, which was expressed, for instance, by the joint formation of the sole list of candidates to elections at all levels.

[9] In an article published in the Warsaw daily *Życie Warszawy* at the turn of 1981 Andrzej Werblan, having then just resigned from his very pronounced position as the Member of the Secretariat of the Central Committee of the Party, pointed out exactly the utmost demoralization resulting from the situation, in which he had been entitled to issue orders to the ministers over the telephone, without bearing any responsibility for it (unless the matter was within the competence of another member of the Secretariat).

acquiring things in a formally proper manner (I was standing in this line), though, perhaps, a bit more effectively, and getting them quite informally is very, very thin indeed, the more so as the mechanism is in both cases the same. This system is, however, far beyond mafia in that it totally shapes and maintains both these ethical codes - the external and the internal ones - on whose difference it preys.

12. The motivation to shortage turns into motivation to inefficiency. There is no reason for producing more, or at a lower cost, if it is power, not economics that matters, and power is gained from shortage. Productivity decreases and thereby full employment is easily assured - nay, even just to secure the optimum shortage of goods there may at some point not be enough labour.[10]

4.3 The change

1. There is a race between the decrease in effectiveness, induced by the "optimum shortage" philosophy, and the increase of employment (this race exists in both the case of population increase and of the progressive use of latent labour resources, if a steady increase of consumption level is assumed). There is an end to this race, of course. But when this end comes, the system is no longer able to cope with the challenge: how to preserve the "optimum shortage" level when there is a shortage of labour. This would require increasing productivity, which nobody (the system) knows how to do any more. And, in fact, there is still sufficiently strong motivation within the system to maintain the optimum shortage philosophy, with the optimum simply having moved down to some lower level.[11]

---

[10] In a distribution-and-shortage system power is proportional to the exchange capacity, which, in turn, is proportional to the length of the queue, or queues, that one is managing, and the importance of goods distributed thereby. Hence also the drive towards the gigantic enterprises, employing thousand and tens of thousands of people: they were the realms of the directors, also nominated, effectively, by the Party, who wanted their power to grow as much as possible, and their workers were their customers or clients (another source of this drive was, of course, the economic ideology of the prevalence of the production of production means and the military complex).

[11] Despite the appearances, this is what has been actually taking place in the European communist countries outside of the Soviet Union in the post-war period: while some new goods entered the market (like TV sets, cars, automatic washing machines, etc.) and their production, as well as consumption, increased, the shortages of some of the staple goods got even more acute (e.g. food products, but also many other products of everyday use, like toilet paper).

2. One of the solutions seems to lie in a massive introduction of foreign resources. And that is what happens quite often, indeed. These resources, however, get easily completely sucked away by the insatiable system of distributors, so that in a short time nothing is left and no enhancement nor improvement occurs.

3. Another solution, perhaps, lies in a change of the principles governing the system.

4. Any attempt at a partial (gradual or smooth) change must of necessity fail, being absorbed and/or annihilated by the system, keeping to the well understood own interest, strictly connected with preservation of the basic features of the system (disposal, shortage, concealed information, personal power, duality, ...).[12]

5. Things may become, however, so bad (the average served proportion of the queue falling down to 60-70 per cent, for instance) that it is, after all, necessary to attempt a complete change of the system. Obviously, for many, the only alternative worth considering is market economy and far-reaching privatisation or re-privatisation of economic assets (even if, in fact, this is by no means the only alternative). When looking closer at it, however, one easily guesses that many of the herring sellers have very little against total privatisation as long as it is being carried out while they are still in positions of power. (Wanna capitalism? Sure, why not - but we gonna be the capitalists.) One of the sources of their motivations is the threat that in conditions of falling efficiency their exchange power may be eroded, or that a revolution may occur, but for some, especially those at relatively low positions and those seeing their perspectives within the system as blind alleys - it is the perspective of better gains and broader possibilities with the new order.[13]

6. Now, privatization may proceed by giving away, by selling, or in a concealed manner as a quasi-managerial revolution, and in all these cases it is herring sellers, their likes and superiors, who are the first ones

---

[12] An illustration for such a self-rectifying action of the system is provided by the attempted reform in Poland at the end of the 1970s. The established Large Economic Organizations (WOGs), mimicking corporations, running altogether some 40 per cent of the Polish economy, were to act relatively independently within the system of definite economic parameters. The entire effort failed completely, because it simply turned into the *distribution of the parameter values*!

[13] The situation, though, is no longer as clean and nice as before. First, the official and unofficial ideology of equality, low effort, possibilities of acquiring beyond the simple work and compensation scheme, has made inroads into the social thinking, even if not quite conscious (after all, it **did cost less**). Second, a part of the distributors are afraid of being left without the safeguarding system. Yet, the change is forced upon the society from both the bottom (the social unrest) and the top (awareness of most of the system leaders).

in the line (or - in the *proper* line). No wonder, it is them who have the resources and power to seize the new opportunity in a well-organized manner. Once there, the herring sellers are mostly interested in preservation of group-monopolistic or oligopolistic economy.

High barriers to market entry, cumbersome laws and paperwork necessary to start a business secure the positions of those, who made it at the very beginning.

7. Thus, a quasi-liberal, oligopolistic economy is established, in which some features of the previous system are preserved, associated, first of all, with the existence of deeply ingrained *do ut des* institution taking the form of widespread corruption, lack of recognition of *moral hazard* and *conflict of interest* situations as disruptive. As long as there are sources of oligopolistic rent, first of all in the quasi-monopolistic sectors, there is also no need for internally generated innovation.

This system is, of course, little sensitive to changes in, say, tax and interest rate policies. It is the consumer and petty business that will pay at the end. Actually, taxation serves mainly to satisfy the political demands and privileges. The clientele of the system develops and takes roots very quickly indeed[14]. Thereby its stability is greatly enhanced.

4.4 Some comments

1. It is true that any system involving (re)distribution is conducive to a certain degree of informal give-and-take and corrupt behaviour. Yet, there is a very distinct, nay - dramatic - difference between the existence of such behaviour in an otherwise democratically and openly functioning society, and the running of the entire society and economy through such a system. The latter system makes altogether not only money worthless, which would be perhaps morally justified (?) by some, but also systematically rewards outward lie and concealed information at any level (what about market studies? opinion polls?), and, while maintaining the myth of (quasi)full employment, leads to complete destruction of work morale.

[14] Already in 1981 a study of the sociologist, Professor Jadwiga Staniszkis, carried out in the large factories in Poland, showed that blue-collar workers wanted socialism to be abolished, but, at the same time, did not want to work in a private enterprise. Then, the first unemployment benefit regulation introduced in Poland after 1989 was so liberal that it encompassed virtually all those non-working, even though most of them never tried to nor wanted to. Yet, they applied en masse for the benefits. Nowadays it is the pure electoral arithmetic that does define the re-distribution.

2. Indeed, the herring barrel system has definite ideological appeal, for the positive reasons mentioned before, as an escape from the rat-race, the commercial greed, etc. It also actively involves quite an important portion of the society, not just the topmost elite: indeed, the system has to be composed of a vast army of distributors, who carry after them their families, even if their exchange power is limited. This is, definitely, one of the pillars of the system's stability, and then longing for it. Yet, the system is most appealing to those potentially in power, who can use the ideological instrument, while establishing a coherent totalitarian regime.

3. Now, it is obvious that the herring barrel system is ultimately a totalitarian one, exercising total control over the society and economy. It is the backbone of the Orwell's *1984*'s image (Orwell, 1949) of the state and society. A very clear distinction, however, must be made between the totalitarian and the authoritarian regimes. Virtually all of the communist countries tried to install and run totalitarian systems, with varying degrees of success. Of the fascist or quasi-fascist regimes it was perhaps Nazi Germany that came closest to the totalitarian scheme. It must be remembered that a totalitarian regime needs not be a physically cruel one, with death squads and (mass) executions. On the contrary, the more totalitarian a system becomes the less physical oppression it needs to exert. After 1956 the tight grip could loosen, because control was already established.

4. The system collapses because of its inherent inefficiency, which becomes more and more acute and visible, both for those in top positions and for those in the lengthening queues. The system, whose sense resides in shortage and personal power, breaks down because of its economic shortcomings. Yet it can endow its "descendant" with certain features that preserve some of the characteristics of informal exchange and power. There should be an acute awareness of both this tendency and its consequences.

5. In this sketch there is little, if any, mention of the otherwise commonly assumed foundations of the socialist/communist system, such as e.g. planned economy, ideology of equality, etc. Likewise, no use is made of the historical roots and development of the communist ideology and practice. The intention was to illustrate the bare mechanism of power and the true internal workings of the system, whatever its origin and face value. In fact, communism was brought to many countries in a variety of ways, in some cases simply by sheer force. The exchange and distribution system of power, with all its unalienable properties, such as shortage, inefficiency, lack of truth, personal power, doublethink, etc., is the unifying tissue of all these incarnations of the communist paradigm.

It is true that most of these features of the system have been noticed and analysed, starting with shortages. This was, in particular, the subject of the famous paper by Janos Kornai (Kornai, 1980, and 1992), who treated shortages as an inherent characteristic of the system. Yet, although his analysis shows precisely all the economic conditions associated with shortage (economy), shortage is not considered to be the *system-forming* aspect.

Similarly, lack of true information is noted by many (see, e.g. Lipton and Sachs, no date), but, again, it is not seen as a *inherent* aspect of the system.

In a positive perspective (wages ... are to be distributed according to the social value of the service performed) emphasis is placed on exactly all those features, which have been (and still from time to time are) officially used to justify communism (or real socialism) and to demonstrate its superiority to the market economy. Whether we speak of just distribution or of gift economy, we deal with ideological constructs, which all fall short of any realistic assessment of implementation and its consequences. Ultimately, virtually all of them rely on the inherent goodness of human nature, and especially of those, who introduce and maintain the system, and who should be exceptionally honest and self-denying. The second flaw is, of course, the assumption of perfect - or close to perfect - knowledge (within the system, but definitely associated with the same leaders) of human needs, technological processes and the like.

These assumptions, though, are very close to the heart of many, who believe that there is a fair pay, fair share and a fair price that is well known to the wise, and only the spitefulness of the wrongdoers prevents from implementing these. This belief is on what ideology and associated politics preys effectively, while tacitly taking away from the faithful any influence on pay, share and price.

That is altogether why dealing away with the communist system is an unprecedented event in European history, and why it is so difficult.

References

Gros, D. and A. Steinherr (2004) *Economic Transition in Central and Eastern Europe: Planting the Seeds*. Cambridge: Cambridge University Press.

Kornai, J. (1980) *Economics of Shortage*. Vol. A, p. 27; Vol. B, p. 196. Amsterdam: North Holland Press.

Kornai, J. (1992) *Socialist Economy*. Princeton, NJ: Princeton University Press.

Lipton, D. and J. Sachs (no date) *The Consequences of Central Planning in Eastern Europe*. http://faculty.vassar.edu/kennett/Lipton.htm

Orwell, G. (1949) *1984*.

Owsiński, J.W. (1992) A Metaphoric System of Economy: The Herring Barrel Metaphor. *Control & Cybernetics*, **21**(2), 23-9.

Part II

Redistribution, Government, Technology, and Human Capital

Chapter 5

Transition and Stability of Redistribution Policies

Jean-Luc Schneider

The chapter presents a simple theoretical model of a society subject to choice, expressed through voting, on a potential move away from the status quo. This move is interpreted in term of choice between (more of) capitalism and (more of) socialism, expressed through parameters corresponding to degree of equality/redistribution and economic effectiveness. Seemingly paradoxical voting behavior patterns, bearing a striking resemblance to some of the actually observed ones, are thereby explained.

5.1 Introduction

This paper addresses the question of how a democracy chooses the level of income redistribution between individuals which is to be implemented in the economy. We argue that, faced with a choice between two systems, even under conditions of perfect foresight at the time of the vote, there is no certainty that a majority of the population select what a majority of the population would agree to be the best system. In other words, a beneficial transition is not ineluctable in a democracy.

To foster such transition, an outside intervention may be needed. For example, a conditional transitory financial support from an external donor may be part of the reform package submitted to the voters. However, although aid can always induce the voters to choose the best system (as well as the worst one), there is no guarantee, in general, that a later vote will not reverse this choice. More strikingly, our model makes it possible that, even without outside intervention, the voters keep oscillating between two systems, both unstable.

In the long-term, and if there is no constraint upon the possible redistribution levels, a democracy converges toward a stable equilibrium system. There is no guarantee that this equilibrium will be unique, and it may depend upon the initial system. But in most cases, full socialism or full capitalism (or both) are stable, even if the majority of the population would have preferred ex-ante a mixed system.

All of these features seem to reflect some of the stylized facts observed in recent years, when a number of countries had to vote on drastic reforms of their economic system, involving thorough changes in redistributive policy. Most initially socialist countries first voted in favor of a much more market-oriented system, accompanied by higher levels of income inequality and better incentives. A considerable number of them later reversed their initial choices.

Such policy reversals are sometimes attributed to disappointment, namely voters either did not realize that the market economy is not all rosy (at the time of the first vote), or did not realize that the transition takes some time to bear fruit (at the time of the second vote). Myopia, if not irrationality would explain their behavior. Instead, our model provides an explanation which is compatible with full rationality and perfect foresight.

5.2 The model

Consider the following continuous time model. At any time t, a continuum of individuals are born, differing only in their initial human capital endowment z. A proportion g of them, the 'gifted' ones, feature a high initial human capital endowment (z=1); the 1-g others are 'non-gifted' (z=0). Each individual lives for one unit of time and g is constant over time. At any time, an individual is identified by his age a and his initial human capital z. There is no demographic growth and the distribution of ages is uniform over [0;1] at any time t.

An individual works all his life and receives a gross income $y(z;a;t)$, varying with age a and skill. At age a, he chooses the level of effort $e(z;a;t)$ which he provides in his work. Effort $e(z;a;t)$ has a utility cost equal to $ce(z;a;t)^2$, where c is a strictly positive coefficient. Effort increases a worker's human capital, denoted by $H(z;a;t)$, which equals the cumulative effort provided during his life up to time t. Human capital enhances workers' gross income, $y(a;z;t)$. Thus, at time t:

$$y(z;a;t) = z + H(z;a;t) \tag{5.1}$$

where:

$$H(z;a;t) = \int_0^a e(z;a;t-a+u)\,du. \tag{5.2}$$

The interest rate equals zero, and there is no financial market (without loss of generality, as long as no taxation of saving is considered). Therefore, all income is consumed immediately. It is assumed that at any time t, an individual $(z;a)$ maximizes his expected utility over his remaining lifetime:

$$U(z;a;t) = \int_0^{1-a} \left[x(z;a+u;t+u) - ce(z;a+u;t+u)^2\right] \mathrm{d}u\,. \tag{5.3}$$

The notion of gifted individuals may reflect various scenarios. For example, it may represent some differences in innate productivity. But z can also be seen as an inherited and exogenous flow of utility, that would affect only some individuals, for example an inherited asset providing some fixed financial income. Similarly, z may capture some geographical discrepancy between favoured and less favoured areas of the same country, in terms of natural resources. Note that in our model all individuals are implicitly risk-neutral.

Let $E(m)$ denote the economy in which at any time t and for any individual $(z;a)$ net income $x(z;a;t)$ is linked to gross income $y(z;a;t)$ through the formula:

$$x(z;a;t) = my(z;a;t) + (1-m)Y_m(t) \tag{5.4}$$

where m is fixed and lies between 0 and 1, and Y_m (t) is the average income per capita in the economy at that time. With this notation, $E(0)$ is a fully egalitarian system, in which all individuals receive the same income, regardless of their productivity. For convenience, this equal income economy will be called 'socialism'. Conversely, $E(1)$ corresponds to an economy in which everyone is paid exactly at one's productivity level. For symmetry reasons, it will be called 'capitalism'. Coefficient m determines workers' exposure to market forces and it measures the level of incentive in the economy. Alternatively, $1\text{-}m$ can be interpreted as the level of social protection against unequal human capital distribution. Needless to mention, the words 'socialism' and 'capitalism', as well as the words 'left' and 'right' that will be employed later, are purely conventional and must only be interpreted in terms of the redistribution parameter m.

In $E(m)$, individual $(z;a)$ provides an additional effort $\mathrm{d}e_m$ during a period of time $\mathrm{d}t$, provided that its cost, that is $2ce_m(z;a;t)\mathrm{d}e_m\mathrm{d}t$, be not higher than its additional expected return, that is $(1\text{-}a)m\mathrm{d}e_m\mathrm{d}t$. Therefore:

$$e_m(z;a;t) = \frac{m}{2c}(1-a)\,. \tag{5.5}$$

The optimal effort level does not depend upon the individual's initial ability and it decreases over his lifetime, down to zero on his very last working day. By summing between ages 0 and a, an individual $(z;a)$'s human capital at time t, $H_m(z;a;t)$, is obtained, as well as his productivity:

$$y_m(z;a;t) = z + \frac{m}{2c}\left(a - \frac{a^2}{2}\right). \tag{5.6}$$

As expected from such a model, any individual's effort, as well as his productivity, increases with the level of incentives m.

Summing productivity over all individuals $(z;a)$ provides the total output Y_m of economy $E(m)$:

$$Y_m = g + \frac{m}{6c}. \tag{5.7}$$

It is useful to simplify notation by defining s as:

$$s = 1 - 6cg\ . \tag{5.8}$$

Equation (5.7) becomes:

$$Y_m = g\left(1 - \frac{m}{1-s}\right). \tag{5.9}$$

Coefficient s can be positive or negative, but it is always less than 1. It measures how total output Y_m reacts to the level of market exposure m. The higher s, the more sensitive Y_m is to the choice of m. Since s is decreasing with c, it can also be interpreted as a measure of exogenous equality: for a given g, a low s means that individual investment in human capital hardly compensates for differences in initial endowment, whereas these differences are easily overcome if s is high. The model is fully parametrized by the pair $(g;s)$.

Let $U_m(z;0;t)$ denote total utility at birth of individual endowed with z under $E(m)$:

$$U_m(z;0;t) = g + m(z-g) + \frac{g}{1-s}\left(m - \frac{m^2}{2}\right). \tag{5.10}$$

From equation (5.10), the preferred m of an individual at birth is derived. It is always 1 for a gifted individual, coinciding with the macroeconomic objective of output maximization, whereas a non-gifted individual always prefers a lower m. Let m^* denote the ex-ante preferred m of a non-gifted individual:

$$m^* = \mathrm{Max}(0; s)\,. \tag{5.11}$$

The lower level of accumulation of human capital compensates for initial inequality, the lower the market exposure wanted ex-ante by the non-gifted. Full socialism (involving the worst macroeconomic outcome) is even preferred ex-ante by the non-gifted to any other system, if s is negative.

The question of what should be considered as the optimal m is a standard social choice problem. The *utilitarian* approach, consisting of maximizing the sum of all individuals' utilities, would select capitalism (m=1) as the optimal system. This would also satisfy the objective of total output maximization. However, it is not completely satisfying, because the implicit argument in favour of the utilitarian approach, according to which, once utility maximization is reached, additional transfers may be used to reach a better distribution of utility across individuals, does not hold in this model where transfers and redistribution are already embodied in the choice of m.

The alternative *Rawlsian* approach, which has the aim of maximizing the utility of the worst-off individual, simply consists of adopting the m which is preferred ex-ante by the non-gifted. In the case where the non-gifted are a majority, the *Rawlsian* approach is consistent with democracy, in the sense that the outcome is the steady state which is preferred ex-ante by a majority of individuals.

It will be assumed thereafter that $g < 1/2$ holds, and m^*, that is the ex-ante choice by a majority which coincides with the ex-ante choice by the non-gifted will also be referred to as the optimal m. Note that the optimal m depends upon s only, and not upon g. It will involve no loss of generality to assume thereafter that s is greater than or equal 0. So m^* and s coincide.

Then, the parameter s is equal to the m which is preferred by a majority of the population, if it were given, at birth, the choice between all possible steady states. Equation (5.10) is more general: it describes the population's ex-ante preferences, and it can be used to select the optimal m inside various sets of offered m's, from a comparative statics point of view. However, the transition problem itself, the voters' choice when offered to shift to a new incentive system in the midst of their working life, still needs to be adressed.

To model the actual vote about a change in m, let us assume that the economy has been $E(m)$ to date 0, and that at time 0 all individuals are (unexpectedly) asked whether they are willing to shift to $E(m')$ from time 0 on or to stay with $E(m)$ forever. If not otherwise indicated, it is assumed that no transfers across generations take place that is, the total output of the economy equals the sum of incomes of all individuals at any given time.

Differences with comparative statics are twofold. First, individuals' history matters since individuals are faced with a new system of incentives but are endowed with the human capital they have accumulated. Therefore, one may benefit in the steady state from the new system, but still be worse off during the transition due to the impossibility to adapt one's human capital to the new conditions. Second, the transition may involve transfers between different age groups. For instance, the young may vote for a more egalitarian society as a means to take advantage of the capital the elderly have accumulated. The model builds upon these ideas.

Let $\Delta m = m' - m$ and $\Delta U(z;a;0)$ be the difference between the total utility of individual z aged a at time 0 under $E(m)$ and under the economy denoted by $TE(m;m')$, which uses m to date 0 and m' afterwards. Note that transition lasts exactly one generation, since the effort level depends only upon the individual's age. As soon as there are no survivors from the old system, the economy reaches a new steady state. Formally, for $t > 1$, $TE(m;m')$ coincides with $E(m')$.

It is easy, but somewhat cumbersome (see Appendix), to derive the change in utility of individual $(z;a)$ if Δm is implemented at time 0:

$$\frac{\Delta U(z;a;0)}{(1-a)\Delta m} = z - g + \frac{g}{8(1-s)}[f_1(a) + mf_2(a) + \Delta m f_3(a)] \tag{5.12}$$

with:

$$f_1(a) = 5 - 3a - 3a^2 + a^3 \tag{5.13}$$

$$f_2(a) = -5 + 11a - a^2 - a^3 \tag{5.14}$$

$$f_3(a) = -1 - 5a + 7a^2 - a^3 . \tag{5.15}$$

5.3 The choice between socialism and capitalism

Let us first focus on choice between full socialism (m=0) and full capitalism (m=1). From a comparative statics point of view, it is clear from equation (5.10) that a non-gifted individual prefers capitalism to socialism if:

$$s > \frac{1}{2} = S_0(g) . \tag{5.16}$$

To see whether this social choice frontier translates into actual votes, suppose that, in a socialist economy, voters are offered the choice of switching to capitalism or retaining socialism. Using equations (5.12) to (5.15) where m is replaced by 0 and Δm by 1, we see that gifted individuals vote for the reform, regardless of their age, but that only the youngest of the non-gifted voters approve of the transition (because $f_1(a)+f_3(a)$ is decreasing in a over [0;1]). Whether or not they form with the gifted voters a majority in favor of the reform depends upon g and s. The reform gets majority approval if:

$$s > 1-\frac{1}{8(1-g)^2} = S_1(g)\,. \tag{5.17}$$

For all g between 0 and 1/2:

$$S_1(g) > \frac{1}{2}\,. \tag{5.18}$$

It is certain that whenever socialism is the optimal steady state, it is also stable against capitalism, in the sense that the shift to capitalism is rejected by a majority of voters. However, there exists also a set of economies (for s between 1/2 and S_1 (g)), which, if initially socialist, will not move to capitalism under a democracy, although there would be a majority of the population to agree ex-ante that capitalism is preferable.

Conversely, if the economy is initially under capitalism (m=1), it can be proved (see Appendix) that all gifted voters vote against a shift to socialism, whereas the non-gifted young vote for the shift, but are never so many as to form a majority. However, for some ($g;s$), the non-gifted young are joined by some or all non-gifted elderly and may add to a majority in favor of socialism. More formally, a majority of the population chooses to move the economy toward socialism (m'=0) if:

$$s < S_2(g) \tag{5.19}$$

where S_2 is an increasing function of g over [0;1/2], always strictly lower than 1/2 (see proof in Appendix).

An interesting point of the model is that the non-gifted young are more prone to radical change than the non-gifted elderly, under both capitalism and socialism. Their behaviour, however, is dictated by different motives:

- During a transition from socialism to capitalism, the non-gifted young have more time to invest in human capital. Thus, the productivity level they reach compensates for harder work and the immediate loss of transfers from gifted workers' production. Elderly non-gifted workers are never able to compensate for these short-term losses.
- During a transition from capitalism to socialism, the non-gifted young vote for the reform because it allows them to confiscate other workers' production. Therefore, they receive transfers both from the gifted workers and from the elderly non-gifted ones. These transfers

combined with the possibility to work less during their entire life, more than compensate for the gradual drop in total output.

Elderly workers tend to be more conservative. A switch to socialism would deprive elderly non-gifted workers from the fruits of previous capital accumulation. Therefore, they vote against the reform. However, under some initial conditions $(g;s)$, very old non-gifted workers may favour socialism against initial capitalism, because they will not suffer from the medium-term fall in total production, but they will somehow benefit from confiscation of the gifted workers' production. This happens when s is low enough, so that under the capitalist regime the difference between gifted and non-gifted workers' productivity far exceeds the difference in productivity between non-gifted young and non-gifted elderly workers.

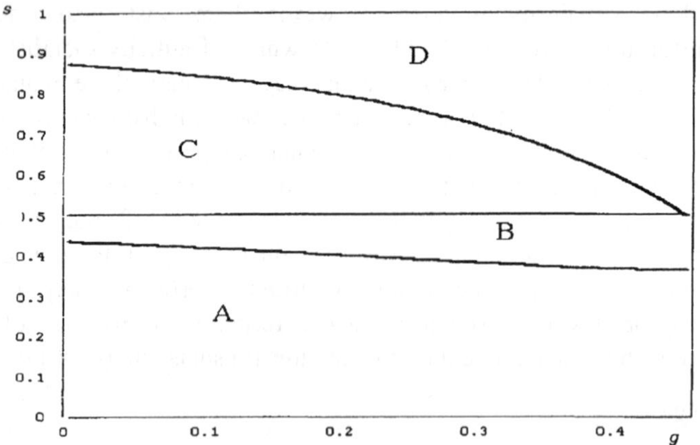

parameter g: proportion of gifted individuals in the population
parameter s: easiness to overcome the initial handicap

Figure 5.1. Choice between socialism and capitalism $m = 0; m' = 1$

Figure 5.1 summarizes the previous results. Socialism (resp. capitalism) is socially optimal in areas A and B (resp. C and D). If the economy is initially socialist (resp. capitalist), a majority of voters vote for keeping socialism (resp. capitalism) against a shift to capitalism (resp. socialism) in areas A, B, and C (resp. B, C and D). In particular, for all $(g;s)$'s in areas B and C, both capitalism and socialism are stable against radical changes. The inertia in the double-equilibrium area implies that the economy may remain in a non-optimal state in spite of a democratic voting game.

This over-stability of possibly suboptimal states provides some grounds to an outside one-time intervention aimed at pushing the economy toward the desired long-term equilibrium. So far, only balanced transition has been considered, in the sense that current consumption equals current output at any time. But one can think of simple intergenerational transfers that would allow to compensate present voters for short-term utility losses, in order to convince a majority of them to go for the reform. The transfer would then be paid back out of the welfare increase of future generations.

5.4 The choice between socialism and a mixed system

The previous section indicated that, faced with a big-bang choice, a democracy may exhibit some excess inertia, relative for to the social optimality criteria. However, it is efficient in two ways: (1) if a reform is voted it is always a good one; and (2) once the economy has got the best of both systems, it retains it.

Unfortunately, in the general case of smaller reforms those comforting results no longer hold. For example, it is easy to calculate $S_0(g)$, $S_1(g)$, and $S_2(g)$, corresponding to m=0 and m'=1/2, which represents the choice between socialism and a mixed system. As in the big-bang case, $S_0(g)$ is defined as the critical s below which m=0 is ex-ante preferred to m=1/2; whereas $S_1(g)$ is the lowest s for which a shift from m=0 to m=1/2 is approved by a majority; and $S_2(g)$ is the highest s for which a shift from m=1/2 to m=0 is approved by a majority. These three curves are drawn in Figure 5.2.

Socialism is optimal in area A, whereas the mixed system is optimal in areas B,C,D, and E. However, if it is proposed that they should shift from socialism to the mixed system, the voters choose socialism in areas A, B, and D, and they a majority vote for the mixed system only in areas C and E. This is the kind of inertia which has already been observed in the big-bang case. But surprisingly, if the economy is initially under the mixed system, a majority of individuals vote to shift to socialism in areas A, B, and C, while they retain the mixed system only in areas D and E. This is inefficient on two grounds.

First, in areas B and C, even though the economy initially stays under the preferred long-term system (here, the mixed system), a majority votes to move away from it. This is because the short-term transfers across individuals which take place during the transition induce a majority of voters to stand for the change to socialism, although they know that this is suboptimal in the long-term. As in the big-bang case, shifting to socialism allows both the young non-gifted and the very old non-gifted to confiscate the human capital accumulated by all the gifted and the middle-aged non-gifted. It is worthwhile to do so even if the economy progressively slows down, because short-term transfers compensate for the reduction in longer-term utility for the young non-gifted, the elderly non-gifted being dead when the bad times come.

Secondly, there may exist endogenous policy instability. If the parameters of the model lie in area C, and if the choice between socialism and the mixed system is proposed repeatedly (at time intervals longer than 1), then each vote reverses the previous one. Area C is characterized by balanced parameters: about half the population is gifted, and the inequality proxy s lies not too far from 1/2 that is the long-term indifference level between capitalism and socialism. Compared to this relatively low differentiation between economic systems, the transition effects become crucial in the formation of a majority. Since the younger non-gifted benefit from a change, regardless of the initial system, they add either to other non-gifted (to go for socialism) or to the gifted (to go for the mixed system), and constitute a majority in favour of a reform.

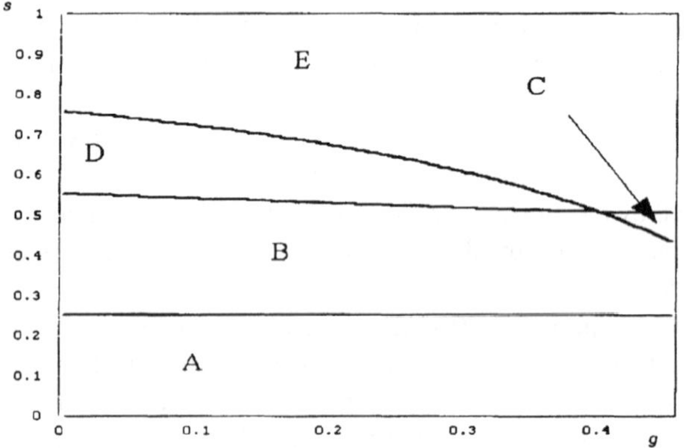

parameter g: proportion of gifted individuals in the population
parameter s: easiness to overcome the initial handicap

Figure 5.2. Choice between socialism and mixed economy $m = 0; m' = 1/2$

While, in the big-bang case, a conditional loan by an outside lender is always able to push the economy toward the preferred steady state, this is no longer the case here. A temporary loan would allow a durable shift from socialism to the mixed system only in area D. In area B, a shift is desirable and could be provoked through a loan, but it would be spontaneously reversed in the next vote. In area C, no loan is necessary to get a desirable shift to the mixed system, but it is unstable.

The situation is quite different in the case of a shift from the mixed system to socialism. If socialism is desirable it is always selected by a majority (for parameters in area A). Moreover, it is stable against a proposal to return to the mixed system. But, starting from the mixed system in area B (where it is optimal), a conditional loan may be able to induce voters to shift to socialism, and they will stick to it thereafter.

Actually, from a static point of view, the economics of the previous examples is simple: once the initial m is fixed, every voter has a single peaked preference function over the possible new m's. Among the m's that are proposed to the voters, he will choose the one which stands closest to his peak. Such preferences have good properties in terms of Arrow's axioms. However, the interesting results of our model stem from the fact that the voter's preferences over the next m depend upon the initial state of the economy, and differ from his long-term preferences. These are the reasons why the dynamics of the model are somewhat more complicated than the standard Arrow's social choice. Continuing in this vein, the next section argues that, in most cases, stability differs from long-term optimality.

5.5 Stability of a redistribution policy

The two previous sections analysed the choice between an incumbent system and a new one, which was exogenously selected and proposed to the voters. It is now natural to wonder which kind of reform Δm is most likely to be proposed to voters living under a given system $E(m)$, and whether there exists a system $E(m)$ such that no reform Δm would ever gain a majority against the existing m. To address these issues, we make four simplifying assumptions:

- Outside interventions (that is non-balanced reform paths) are ruled out.
- Only two-sided choices are proposed to the voters, say the government program and the opposition program.
- The government program consists in keeping the existing system $E(m)$.
- The objective of the opposition is to get as many votes as possible.

With these assumptions, the opposition program consists in proposing the smallest possible reform, either positive or negative. This is an obvious consequence of equations (5.12) to (5.15), once noticed that f_3 is negative over $[0;1]$. The direction of the opposition program is given by the sign of Δm. To compute the adequate sign, the right hand side of equation (12) must be computed with Δm taken equal to zero, denoted by, say, $V(z;a)$:

$$V(z;a) = z - g + \frac{g}{8(1-s)}[f_1(a) + mf_2(a)]. \tag{5.20}$$

For a given pair of parameters $(g;s)$ and a given m, this is either positive or negative for each $(z;a)$. Let $L(m;g;s)$ denote the proportion of pairs $(z;a)$ for which $V(z;a)$ is positive. Then the opposition program is the smallest possible Δm with the sign of $L(m;g;s)$-1/2, that is, the sign taken by $V(z;a)$ for a majority of $(z;a)$'s, provided that it be feasible.

In other words, if the opposition differentiates itself as little as possible from the government in the right direction, then it will maximize its constituency. If the opposition is unable to reach a majority with a very small reform program, it is unable to win with any reform program at all, and the existing system $E(m)$ is called an equilibrium system.

Equilibrium systems can take three forms:

- If the opposition program requires that $\Delta m<0$, while m already equals 0, then socialism is an equilibrium. This happens if $L(0;g;s)<1/2$.
- If the opposition program requires that $\Delta m>1$, while m already equals 1, then capitalism is an equilibrium. This happens if $L(1;g;s)>1/2$.
- If b, g, and s are such that $V(z;a)$ is positive for exactly half the $(z;a)$'s, then $E(m)$ is an equilibrium. This happens if $L(m;g;s)=1/2$.

The last category can be divided into two sub-categories, according to the sign of the expression:

$$\frac{\partial L}{\partial m}(m;g;s)\,. \tag{5.21}$$

If expression (5.21) is greater than zero, then any exogenous change in the initial system $E(m)$ would result in later divergence from $E(m)$. The equilibrium system $E(m)$ is then said to be unstable. Instead, if expression (5.21) is lower than zero, the equilibrium system $E(m)$ exhibits stability in the sense that a vote would push the economy back toward $E(m)$ in case of a small initial parting from it. With this definition, socialism (resp. capitalism) is always stable if it is an equilibrium system.

It results from the continuity of V in a, m, g, and s (and from the fact that $V(1;a) > 0$ for all a's) that L is also continuous in m, g, and s. Therefore, there exists at least one stable equilibrium $E(m)$ for every pair of parameters $(g;s)$. Moreover, two stable equilibria are always separated by an unstable equilibrium.

Under the previous assumptions (and still supposing that nobody ever votes more than once in a lifetime), starting from any m_0, the political dynamics of a democracy would be to converge slowly through very small reforms towards a stable equilibrium system m^{**} corresponding to its exogenous parameters $(g;s)$. If there exist several stable equilibria, the evolution of the system depends on the position of the initial m_0 relative to the unstable equilibria which act as cut-off points between consecutive pairs of stable equilibria.

Socialism is a stable equilibrium if and only if:

$$s \leq 1 - \frac{1}{8} f_1\left(\frac{1-2g}{2-2g}\right). \tag{5.22}$$

Similarly, capitalism is strongly stable if and only if:

$$s \geq 1 - \left(\frac{3-4g}{8(1-g)^2}\right). \tag{5.23}$$

Figure 5.3 represents the areas delimited by equations (5.20) and (5.21). Socialism is stable in areas A and C, while capitalism is stable in areas C and D.

Only for a relatively small set of parameters, namely in area B, is either socialism or capitalism a stable system. For most parameters, either capitalism or socialism is stable against any proposal of reform. This is true, although the optimal m^*, on which a majority would have agreed ex-ante, equals s that is generically a mixed system. This can be seen as an ex-post justification for having first concentrated on the big-bang choice.

There exist some pairs $(g;s)$, in area C, for which both capitalism and socialism are stable. For these pairs of parameters, by continuity of L, there exists an unstable equilibrium strictly between 0 and 1.

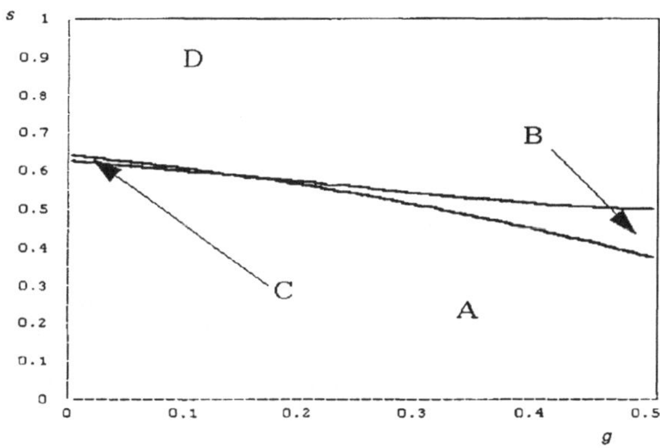

parameter g: proportion of gifted individuals in the population
parameter s: easiness to overcome the initial handicap

Figure 5.3. Stability of capitalism and socialism

Consequently, at least in this area, knowing the exogenous parameters $(g;s)$ is not sufficient to predict the long-term equilibrium of a democracy, which may end under either extreme systems (and, maybe, also under a mixed system) depending up on its starting point.

This opens some new scope for an outside intervention. Among the several stable equilibria, there is one which is preferred by a majority of individuals. By equation (5.10), it is the one which stands closest to s, let it be denoted by m^{**}. But, the actual stable equilibrium may not be m^{**}. An unambiguously useful role for a benevolent outsider would be to push the economy close enough to m^{**}, so that it converge later to the right stable equilibrium. Of course, it is even better, but also more costly, to push it directly to m^{**}. The point is that the target of an outside intervention should not be the ex ante optimal $m^{*}=s$ which is generically not an equilibrium, but the best stable equilibrium m^{**}

In particular, in many cases, the target of the outside intervention would rightly be set at full capitalism or full socialism ($m^{**}=0$ or $m^{**}=1$), although it is clear that neither is the optimal system $E(m^{*})$.

5.6 Conclusion

By developing a very simple model of majority choice with overlapping generations, we were able to rationalize some of the seemingly inconsistent facts observed in the introduction. The basic statement of the chapter is that there is no mechanical coincidence between what an individual regards as the best redistribution level in a steady state, and what he will choose if he is asked to vote in the midst of his life. As a first consequence, no asymmetric information, no bounded rationality, and no changes in preferences are needed to explain why a democracy may remain under a suboptimal redistribution system, or even oscillate between different systems.

The shortcomings of the model are many and are a result of its simplicity. But it should be stressed that the absence of financial markets does not involve any loss of generality. Assuming that individuals could freely reallocate their consumption over their life-cycle would not affect our results as long as no taxation of savings is considered. The possibility of borrowing during youth would not alter the incentive to accumulate human capital, neither the human capital stock at the time of the unexpected choice. As a consequence, the difference in utility under two different systems would be the same with or without savings.

Therefore, the impossibility of any dissociation between the tax system and the career profile is less of an inconvenience than it could have at first appeared. Even though any change in the redistribution schedule affects simultaneously the wealth sharing between the young and the elderly and between the gifted and the non-gifted, the former could be corrected by a financial market which would not affect the issue of the votes.

Still, the model does not include the possibility of measures specifically directed towards an age-category of the population. By compensating the elderly for the inconvenience of a change, such measures would be particularly effective in gaining the approval of a majority at a lower cost than the univeral transfer considered in the model. As long as the transfer to the elderly is financed out of external borrowing, it would be easy to incorporate in the model in order to calculate the minimum external cost of securing approval of a reform. But sometimes, the transfer to the elderly could be financed directly out of the increase in domestic resources stemming from the adoption of a reform. Such self-reliant reform would, of course be preferred to an external aid which might push the economy in the wrong direction. However, it would no longer involve a vote on a one-dimensional parameter (the m of the model), since the text submitted to the electorate would also have to include the amount of the transfer to the elderly, the age above which it would apply, and for how long. The complexity of the choice is likely to obscure the results of our simplistic model.

More disturbingly, we do not know how to model votes occurring at intervals shorter than one generation. Although the model would allow the consideration of such votes at high computation costs, it would not provide any hint about the choice of the sequence of proposals submitted to the voters. Still, a prior about future choices would be necessary to calculate the issue of the first vote, at least for those voters who face a non-zero probability to have to vote again. Taking this into account would lead the model far beyond its initial scope and result in likely multiple dynamic equilibria.

References

Alesina A., D. Rodrik (1994) Distributive Politics and Economic Growth. *Quarterly Journal of Economics*, **109**, 465-90.

Benabou R. (1996) Heterogeneity, Stratification and Growth. *American Economic Review*, **86**, 584-609.

Benabou R. (1996) Unequal Societies. *CEPR Discussion Paper*, 1419.

Fernandez R. and D. Rodrik (1991) Resistance to Reform: Status Quo Bias in the Presence of Individual-Specific Uncertainty. *American Economic Review*, **81**, 1146-1155.

Kuznets S. (1955) Economic Growth and Income Inequality. *American Economic Review*, **45**, 1-28.

Levy F. and R. Murnane (1992) U.S. Earnings Levels and Earnings Inequality: A Review of Recent Trends and Explanations. *Journal of Economic Literature*, **30**, 1333-1381.

Little A. (1984) Education, Earnings and Productivity: The Eternal Triangle. In J. Oxenham, *Education Versus Qualification*? G. London: Allen and Unwin.

Mincer J. (1958) Investment in Human Capital and Personal Income Distribution. *Journal of Political Economy*, **66**, 281-302.

Perotti R. (1993) Political Equilibrium, Income Distribution and Growth. *Review of Economic Studies*, **60**, 755-76.

Piketty T. (1995) Social Mobility and Redistributive Politics. *Quarterly Journal of Economics*, **110**, 551-84.

Saint-Paul G. and T. Verdier (1993) Education, Democracy and Growth. *Journal of Development Economics*, **42**, 399-407.

Shiller R., M. Boycko and V. Korobov (1991) Popular Attitudes Toward Free Markets: The Soviet Union and the United States Compared. *American Economic Review*, **81**, 385-400.

Appendix

A5.1 Proof of Equations (5.12) to (5.15)

Let $\Delta m = m' - m$. For all t, quantities with subscript m refer to the corresponding steady state quantities in $E(m)$. For $t > 0$, quantities with subscript m' refer to the quantities in the economy $TE(m;m')$ which uses m till date 0 and m' afterwards. A quantity preceded by Δ denotes the difference between this quantity with subscript m' and the same quantity with subscript m. Note that for $t > 1$, $TE(m;m')$ coincides with $E(m')$: as soon as there are no longer individuals who have lived under the old system, the economy reaches its new steady state (this is due to the fact that effort level only depends on the individual's age). In other words, the transition lasts exactly one generation. Since we are only interested in the choice of individuals alive at time 0, all subsequent equations are written for $0 < t < 1$.
With this notation:

$$e_m(z;a;t;) = \frac{3g}{(1-s)} m(1-a) + \frac{3g}{1-s} \Delta m(1-a) \tag{5.24}$$

from which the human capital level is derived by summing:

$$H_{m'}(z;a;t;) = H_m(z;a;t) + \int_0^t e_{m'}(z;a-t+x;x)\mathrm{d}x\,. \tag{5.25}$$

That is:

$$H_{m'}(z;a;t) = \frac{3g}{2(1-s)} m(2a-a^2) + \frac{3g}{2(1-s)} \Delta m(2t-2at+t^2)\,. \tag{5.26}$$

And summing productivity over all individuals $(z;a)$ at time t gives total output at time t:

$$Y_{m'}(t) = g + \int_0^1 H_{m'}(z;x;t)\mathrm{d}x\,. \tag{5.27}$$

That is:

$$Y_{m'}(t) = g + \frac{g}{1-s} m + \frac{g}{2(1-s)} \Delta m(3t-t^2)\,. \tag{5.28}$$

Let $u_m(z;a;t)$ and $u_{m'}(z;a;t)$ be the instantaneous utilities at time t of an individual with ability z and aged a under $E(m)$ and $TE(m;m')$

respectively, and let $\Delta u(z;a;t)$ denote their difference. With simplified notations:

$$\Delta u = \Delta m(y-Y) + m(\Delta y - \Delta Y) + \Delta Y - \frac{(1-s)e\Delta e}{3g} +$$

$$+ \Delta m(\Delta y - \Delta Y) - \frac{(1-s)\Delta e^2}{6g}. \tag{5.29}$$

By replacing $H_j(z,a,t)$, $Y_j(t)$, and $e_j(z;a;t)$, and for $j = m, m'$ in Δu $(z;a;t)$, one gets:

$$\begin{aligned}\Delta u(z;a;t) = \Delta m(z-\gamma) + \frac{g}{2(1-s)}\Delta m(3t-t^2) \\ + \frac{g}{2(1-s)} b\Delta m(-8+18a-9a^2+3t-6at+3t^2+t^3) \\ + \frac{3g}{(1-s)}\Delta m^2(-3+6a-3a^2+3t-6at+3t^2+t^3).\end{aligned} \tag{5.30}$$

The expected utility of individual $(z;a)$ at time 0 under $TE(m;m')$ is given by:

$$\Delta U(z;a;o) = \int_0^{1-a} \Delta u(z;a;+x;x)\mathrm{d}x. \tag{5.31}$$

That is:

$$\begin{aligned}\frac{\Delta U(z;a;0)}{(1-a)\Delta m} = z - g + \frac{g}{8(1-s)}(5-3a-3a^2+a^3) \\ + \frac{g}{8(1-s)} m(-5+11a-a^2-a^3) \\ + \frac{g}{8(1-s)}\Delta m(-1-5a+7a^2-a^3).\end{aligned} \tag{5.32}$$

A5.2 Proof of equation (5.19)

Suppose that voters are offered to move from capitalism to socialism. By putting m equal to 1 and Δm to -1 in equation (5.10), it turns out that individual $(z;a)$ is better off after the change if:

$$z - g + \frac{g}{8(1-s)} g(a) < 0 \tag{5.33}$$

with:

$$G(a) = 1 + 13a - 11a^2 + a^3 . \tag{5.34}$$

Since $G(a)$ is strictly positive over $[0;1]$, all gifted individuals $(z = 1)$ vote against the change to socialism. Non-gifted voters $(z = 1)$ approve of the change if:

$$G(a) < 8(1 - s) . \tag{5.35}$$

$G(a)$ is increasing from $a = 0$ for which $G(0) = 1$, to a_0, and decreasing from a_0 to $a = 1$, for which $G(1) = 4$ *. Let a_1 be the unique solution between 0 and a_0 of $G(1/2) > 4$, we know that $a_1 < 1/2$. Different cases should be distinguished:

- If $s > 7/8$, then equation (31) is never satisfied and everybody votes against the reform.
- If $1/2 < s < 7/8$, the young vote for the change up to certain age $a_2(\sigma)$ which is certainly lower than a_1, hence also than 1/2. Therefore the reform is rejected.
- If $1 - G(a_0)/8 < s < 1/2$, two distinct groups of non-gifted voters approve the reform: the young up to a certain age $a_2(s)$, and the elderly above a certain age $a_3(s)$, were a_2 is increasing in s, and a_3 is decreasing in s. The change is approved if and only if:

$$(1 - g)[a_2(s) + 1 - a_3(s)] > \frac{1}{2} \tag{5.36}$$

that is:

$$a_3(s) - a_2(s) < \frac{1 - 2g}{2 - 2g} . \tag{5.37}$$

- If $s < 1 - G(a_0)/8$, all non-gifted voters approve of the change and they form a majority.

Therefore, there exists a continuous function S_2 over $[0;1/2]$ such that the change from capitalism to socialism is approved if and only if:

$$s > S_2(g) . \tag{5.38}$$

---

* $a_o = \dfrac{11 - \sqrt{82}}{3} \approx 0.648$ and $G(a_o) = \dfrac{-1348 + 164\sqrt{82}}{27} \approx 5.077$

S_2 is obtained by solving equation (5.32) where the inequality is replaced by equality. Let u be its right-hand side. By definition, $S_2(g)$ is such that there exists a_2 such that:

$$G(a_2) = 8(1 - S_2(g)) \tag{5.39}$$

and:

$$G(a_2 + u) = 8(1 - S_2(g)) . \tag{5.40}$$

By subtraction, a_2 must satisfy:

$$3a_2^2 + (3u - 22)a_2 + (u^2 - 11u + 13) = 0 \tag{5.41}$$

and it lies between 0 and 1. Consequently:

$$a_2 = \frac{22 - 3u - \sqrt{328 - 3u^2}}{6} \tag{5.42}$$

from which $S_2(g)$ is obtained by equation (5.34). S_2 is decreasing in g and:

$$S_2\left(\frac{1}{2}\right) = 1 \frac{G(a_0)}{8} . \tag{5.43}$$

This is because a higher proportion of gifted individuals, all voting against the change, involves that more of the non-gifted votes are required to have the reform adopted, corresponding to a lower s, by equation (5.30). If almost half of the population is gifted, then socialism is chosen only if all the non-gifted vote in its favor, which is the case if s is lower than $1 - G(a_0)/8$, by definition of a_0.

The lower bound of S_2 is attained for $g = 0$. It verifies:

$$S_2(0) < \tfrac{1}{2} . \tag{5.44}$$

More precisely, for $g = 0$, one gets $a_2 = \dfrac{41 - \sqrt{1309}}{12} \approx 0.402$ and $s = 1 - \dfrac{G(a_2)}{8} \approx 0.436$.

Chapter 6

Fiscal Policy and Transition: The Case of Poland

Scott Baier and Gerhard Glomm

In this chapter, a version of the Cass-Koopmans economy is used for the purpose of studying the impact of fiscal policy changes on capital accumulation. The focus of the study is on transitional dynamics. It is shown that even moderate change in fiscal policy can have sizeable level effects on income levels along the transition path.

6.1 Introduction

One of the central problems faced by the transition economies of Eastern Europe is to determine which economic activities can be carried out in a decentralized fashion through markets and which through government. One economic activity which is carried out by governments even in western economies is the provision of public goods such as police protection, national defence, public-sector R&D, and so on. Even once it is agreed that the government should provide such public goods, there is still the issue of how much of the public good should be provided and how should it be financed.

This chapter is an attempt to make a contribution to this question by studying a model of an economy in which a government provides a particular type of public good. Broadly speaking, we are addressing the question: What are the effects of government provision of this public good on capital accumulation? The model we use to study this issue is a version of the Cass-Koopmans economy where private households own all (save one) factors of production and supply these factors to the firms. Firms use these factors of production to produce a single consumption good. Since households own the stock of capital, they make all the investment decisions.

In this economy we introduce a government, which collects taxes on labour and capital income at uniform but potentially differing rates. The tax revenue is used for two purposes: (i) investment in capital stock and (ii) lump-sum transfers to households. The government capital stock is thought to have public goods properties. In each period the government budget is balanced.

In section 6.3 we solve for the steady-state and perform comparative statics exercises on the steady-state. We show that:

(i) Holding the overall government size and the composition of the government budget constant, the steady-state level of income is declining in the capital income tax rate.
(ii) Holding the overall government size and the tax rates fixed, the steady-state level of income is rising in the fraction of the public budget allocated to investment.
(iii) Holding the ratio of the two tax rates and the fraction of the government allocated to public investment fixed, the steady-state level of income is hump-shaped in the overall size of the government.

In section 6.4 we solve numerically for the transition path under various public policies. We find that relatively modest policy changes can have sizeable level effects. Section 6.5 contains our concluding remarks.

This chapter complements a large and growing literature on the effects of fiscal policy on capital accumulation in dynamic general equilibrium models. Barro (1990) and Glomm and Ravikumar (1994) provided some early theoretical results about the relationship between fiscal policy and growth. Lucas (1990) and Stokey and Rebelo (1995) find very small growth effects of very drastic changes in fiscal policy, while King and Rebelo (1990), and Jones, Manuelli and Rossi (1993) find sizeable growth effects. Most of this literature focuses on balanced growth equilibria and ignores transitional dynamics. In this chapter we concentrate on the transitional dynamics.

Our model is intended to be an abstraction of a typical post-Soviet economy in Central Europe, such as Poland. When we say that this is an abstraction, we mean that many features of the actual processes of the transition in the Central European economies are excluded from the model. We have abstracted from human capital accumulation, from sectoral reallocation and from partial and gradual privatization. We make these abstractions in order to focus on what changes in fiscal policy do to the level of capital accumulation. Leaving all these other aspects of reform and transition out of our model allows us to study how fiscal policy reform in a Central European country impacts on growth, holding all the other aspects of the transition constant. This corresponds to the *ceteris paribus* assumption which is characteristic of economic theorizing. At this stage, we are unable to carry out an empirical analysis of growth and fiscal policy in Poland as there are too few observations since the fall of communism.

6.2 The model

The economy is populated by a large number of identical individuals who live forever. Preferences are given by

$$\sum_{t=0}^{\infty}\beta^{t}\frac{1}{1-\sigma}\left[c_t^{\psi}(1-n_t)^{1-\psi}\right]^{1-\sigma},\ \sigma>0,\quad 0<\beta<1,\qquad 0<\psi\leq 1,$$

where c_t is consumption at time t and $1\text{-}n_t$ is leisure at time t. In later sections we allow ψ=1; in this case labour is supplied inelastically. More generally, though, ψ is different from unity, so that labour supply is elastic. The production technology is given by

$$y_t = AG_t^{\theta}k_t^{\alpha}n_t^{1-\alpha},\quad A>0,\quad 0<\theta<1,\quad 0<\alpha<1,$$

where k_t is the private capital stock, n_t is employment, G_t is the public capital stock and y_t is output in period t. This technology was used by Barro (1990), Glomm and Ravikumar (1994) in related theoretical work. In those reports the restriction $\theta+\alpha=1$ was imposed to obtain persistent growth. If capital's share of income, α, is in the neighbourhood of 40 per cent, then this restriction requires the output elasticity with respect to public capital to be about 0.6. Such a value exceeds the highest estimates of θ by about 50 per cent (for evidence on the size of θ see Fernald, 1996; Holtz-Eakin, 1994; Evans and Karras, 1994; Hulten and Schwab, 1991; Nadiri and Mamuneas, 1994; Ai and Cassou, 1993; Finn, 1994; and Lynde and Richmond, 1993a,b). In this chapter we do not impose the restriction that $\theta+\alpha=1$. This implies that we obtain convergence to a steady-state in levels. Since θ and α are not required to add up to one we can experiment with various values of available estimates of θ.

Physical capital accumulates according to

$$k_{t+1}=(1-\delta_k)k_t+i_t,\quad 0<\delta_k<1$$

while public capital accumulates according to

$$G_{t+1}=(1-\delta_G)G_t+I_t,\qquad 0<\delta_G<1.$$

The government raises a tax on labour income at the uniform rate τ_L and on capital income at the uniform rate τ_k. A part of the government tax revenue R_t is used to fund investment in public capital I_t; the rest of the tax revenue is used for lump-sum transfers T_t. Since the government is not allowed to borrow, the government's budget constraint is

$$R_t = I_t + T_t.$$

Both households and firms behave competitively, taking as given all prices and the fiscal policy parameters. Households solve the problem

$$\max_{\{c_t, n_t k_{t+1}\}_{t=0}^{\infty}} \sum_{t=0}^{\infty} \beta^t \frac{1}{1-\sigma}\left[c_t^{\psi}(1-n_t)^{1-\psi}\right]^{1-\sigma}$$

$$\text{s.t. } \sum p_t(c_t + k_{t+1} - (1-\delta_k)k_t) = \sum_{t=0}^{\infty} p_t[(1-\tau_L)w_t n_t + (1-\tau_k)q_t k_t] + \pi + T$$

$$\text{given } \{p_t, w_t, q_t\}_{t=0}^{\infty}, (\tau_L, \tau_k), \pi, T,$$

where w_t is the real wage at time t, q_t is the rental rate of capital at time t and p_t is the price of the consumption good at time t relative to the consumption good at time 0. In this case p_t / p_{t+1} is the real interest rate at time t. Here π and T denote the present value of profits and lump-sum transfers, respectively.

Since the capital stock is owned by the households, firms solve purely static profit maximization problems. The profit maximization problem is

$$\max_{\{y_t, n_t^d, k_t^d\}} y_t - w_t n_t^d - q_t k_t^d$$

$$\text{s.t. } y_t = AG_t^{\theta} k_t^{\alpha} n_t^{1-\alpha}$$

$$\text{given } \{w_t, q_t, G_t\}.$$

Total government revenue in period t is

$$R_t = \tau_L w_t n_t + \tau_k q_t k_t.$$

Using the Cobb-Douglas assumption on technology we can write

$$R_t = ((1-\alpha)\tau_L + \alpha\tau_k)y_t.$$

Denoting by $s=(1-\alpha)\tau_L + \alpha\tau_k$ the government's share of GNP and by Δ the fraction of the public budget allocated to investment (rather than transfers) we can write down the law of motion for public capital as

$$G_{t+1} = (1-\delta_G)G_t + \Delta s A G_t^{\theta} k_t^{\alpha} n_t^{1-\alpha}.$$

A competitive equilibrium for this economy is an allocation for the household $\{c_t, n_t, k_{t+1}\}_{t=0}^{\infty}$, an allocation for the firm $\{y_t, n_t^d, k_t^d\}_{t=0}^{\infty}$, prices $\{p_t, w_t, q_t\}_{t=0}^{\infty}$, and public capital sequence $\{G_{t+1}\}_{t=0}^{\infty}$ satisfying

(i) $\{c_t, n_t, k_{t+1}\}_{t=0}^{\infty}$ solves the household's problem,

(ii) $\{y_t, n_t^d, k_t^d\}_{t=0}^{\infty}$ solves the firm's problems,

(iii) $c_t + k_{t+1} - (1-\delta_k)k_t = (1-\Delta s)y_t$

$$n_t = n_t^d$$

$$k_t = k_t^d,$$

(iv) $G_{t+1} = (1-\delta_G)G_t + \Delta s y_t$.

In this definition, the first two conditions are rationality requirements. Condition (iii) imposes market clearing in the consumption goods market, the labour market and the capital market. Goods market clearing takes into account that a fraction of output, Δ*s*, is used for public investment purposes. When there are transfers to households, the fraction (1-Δ*s*) of output is available for private consumption and investment. Alternatively, when part of government revenue is tossed into the ocean, the fraction (1-Δ) of output is available for private use.

6.3 Steady-state analysis

In this section we solve for the steady-state equilibrium. We begin by setting ψ=1, the case of inelastic labour supply. The first order condition for the household's choice of capital in period (*t*+1) is the Euler equation

$$c_t^{-\sigma} = \beta c_{t+1}^{-\sigma}[(1-\tau_k)q_{t+1} + 1 - \delta_k].$$

Profit-maximization by the firm implies, in equilibrium,

$$q_t = \alpha G_t^{\theta} k_t^{\alpha-1}$$

$$w_t = (1-\alpha)G_t^{\theta} k_t^{\alpha}.$$

We can thus write the Euler equation as

$$\left(\frac{c_{t+1}}{c_t}\right)^{\sigma} = \beta\left[(1-\tau_k)\alpha G_{t+1}^{\theta} k_{t+1}^{\alpha-1} + 1 - \delta_k\right].$$

In the steady-state we have $c_{t+1}=c_t=c$, $k_{t+1}=k_t=k$, $G_{t+1}=G_t=G$, $y_{t+1}=y_t=y$. Then the Euler equation yields in the steady-state

$$1=\beta[(1-\tau_k)\alpha G^{\theta}k^{\alpha-1}+1-\delta_k]. \tag{6.1}$$

The law of motion for public capital in steady-state implies

$$G=\left(\frac{\Delta s}{\delta_G}\right)^{\frac{1}{1-\theta}}k^{\frac{\alpha}{1-\theta}}. \tag{6.2}$$

Substituting equation (6.2) into (6.1) yields

$$1=\beta\left[(1-\tau_k)\alpha\left(\frac{\Delta s}{\delta_G}\right)^{\frac{\theta}{1-\theta}}k^{\frac{\alpha\theta}{1-\theta}+\alpha-1}+1-\delta_k\right]. \tag{6.3}$$

We then have

Proposition 1

(*i*) *For Δ and s fixed, the steady-state capital stock increases in the capital tax rate τ_k.*
(*ii*) *For τ_k and s fixed, the steady-state level of capital increases in Δ.*
(*iii*) *For Δ and τ_L/τ_k fixed, the steady-state level of capital is hump-shaped in s, reaching a maximum at θ.*

This result follows immediately from differentiating equation (6.3).

The intuition behind this result is obvious: since capital accumulation is elastic in the long run and labour is supplied perfectly in elastically, public revenue should be raised by taxing labour at a higher rate than capital. In fact, as far as optimal taxes are concerned, the following is true in this model. First, the government should collect as much as possible from the labour tax and use the capital tax (if at all) only to finance the remainder. Second, it may even be optimal to tax labour and to subsidize capital. Also, since increasing Δ raises the marginal product of capital, increasing Δ raises the incentive to invest and thus the rate at which capital is accumulated. Finally, the third part of this proposition is an extension of results in Barro (1990) and Glomm and Ravikumar (1994).

Proposition 2

(*i*) *For Δ and s fixed, the steady-state stock of public capital decreases in the capital tax rate τ_k.*

(*ii*) *For τ_k and s fixed, the steady-state stock of public capital decreases in Δ.*

(*iii*) *For Δ and τ_L/τ_k fixed, the steady-state level of public capital increases in s if $\frac{dk}{d\tau_k} > -\frac{k}{\alpha\tau}$ and decreases in s if $\frac{dk}{d\tau_k} < -\frac{k}{\alpha\tau}$.*

Proposition 2 follows directly from Proposition 1 and equation (6.2). By lowering the tax rate on capital income, the capital stock is raised, and, holding other things equal, so is output. This raises tax revenue which, in turn, raises public investment. The second part of Proposition 2 follows directly from the fact that increasing Δ increases the capital stock (see Proposition 1), which increases tax revenues and since a larger fraction of tax revenues goes toward infrastructure investment, public capital accumulates at a faster rate.

Next, we state how the steady-state level of output depends upon fiscal policy.

Proposition 3

(*i*) *For Δ and s fixed, steady-state output is a decreasing function of the capital tax rate τ_k.*

(*ii*) *For τ_k and s fixed, steady-state output decreases in Δ.*

(*iii*) *For Δ and τ_L/τ_k fixed, steady-state output is a hump-shaped function of s.*

This follows from rearranging equations (6.1) and (6.2) to get

$$Y = \left[\frac{\Delta(\alpha\tau_k - (1-\alpha)\tau_L)}{\delta_G}\right]^{\frac{\theta}{1-\alpha-\theta}} \left[\frac{\beta\alpha(1-\tau_k)}{1-\beta(1-\delta_k)}\right]^{\frac{\alpha}{1-\alpha-\theta}}$$

and differentiating as in Propositions 1 and 2.

6.4 Transitions

In this section we study the impact of fiscal policy changes on the transition path. Focusing on the transition path is perhaps more appropriate for the Eastern European economies than for the USA. In the USA, growth of real per capita output has hovered around 2 per cent for most of the twentieth century (see, for example, Barro, 1993, or Stokey and Rebelo, 1995). For such an economy the classical policy experiments using models which permit balanced growth equilibria as conducted by

Lucas (1990), King and Rebelo (1990), Glomm and Ravikumar (1994), Stokey and Rebelo (1995), are appropriate.

The Eastern European economies cannot boast of such persistent growth performance. After the demise of communism, output dropped, in some cases precipitously. In many countries the trough occurred sometime in the early to mid 1990s and economic recovery set in thereafter. For a description of this transition, see, for example, Fischer, Sahay and Végh (1996). In Poland in 1994, for example, growth of output, adjusted for inflation, was 7 per cent. This growth experience should probably not be considered steady-state or balanced growth, but rather growth during a transition toward a steady-state.

The three equations to be solved are

$$\left(\frac{c_{t+1}}{c_t}\right)^{\sigma} = \beta\left[(1-\tau_k)\alpha A G_{t+1}^{\theta} k_{t+1}^{\alpha-1} + 1 - \delta_k\right] \tag{6.4}$$

$$G_{t+1} = \Delta s A G_t^{\theta} k_t^{\alpha} + 1 - \delta_G \tag{6.5}$$

$$(1-s)y_t = c_t + k_{t+1} - (1-\delta_k)k_t\,. \tag{6.6}$$

Here equation (6.4) is simply the Euler equation for the household's problem with the profit-maximizing condition from the firm's problem which equates the price of capital to the marginal product of capital. Equation (6.5) is the law of motion for public capital, once it is recognized that Δs is the fraction of GNP allocated to public investment.

In the resource constraint in equation (6.6) (1-s) is the fraction of GNP available to the private sector for consumption c_t and investment $i_t = k_{t+1} - (1-\delta)k_t$. The assumption in (6.6) is that the part of the government revenue which is not used for public investment is tossed into the ocean or, alternatively, used for provision of a public good which does not appear explicitly in the model.

Had we used the assumption that part of the public revenue, instead of being tossed into the ocean, is rebated to households as lump-sum transfers, then equation (6.6) would become $(1-\Delta s)y_t = c_t + k_{t+1} - (1-\delta_k)k_t$. We have carried out all our computations under this assumption as well, though. The results for output growth are similar in both versions of the model. Of course, the results for the level of consumption will differ in the two versions of the model.

We are unable to solve this system of difference equations analytically and therefore provide numerical solutions. The parameter values we choose for this exercise are chosen so that the model economy resembles a European transition economy, such as Poland, in some important aspects.

Choosing parameters like these to mimic a definite transition economy is a bit problematic. The typical practice in 'calibration' exercises like this for Western economies is to pick parameters for preferences and technologies so that endogenous variables in the model match the observed values in some long-run average sense. In the real business-cycle literature, for example, the coefficient α is chosen to match capital's share of income from the National Income and Product Accounts averaged over such periods as 30 or 40 years. For the transition economies matching long-run averages is impossible since long-run data are not available.

Table 6.1 Preference, technology and endowment parameters

Discount factor β	0.96
(Inverse) Elasticity of substitution in preferences σ	2
Share parameter in preferences ψ	1
Capital's share of income α	1/3
Elasticity of output with respect to public capital θ	0.1
Scale parameter A	1
Depreciation of private capital δ_k	0.1
Depreciation of public capital δ_G	0.1

Table 6.2 Policy parameters used as a benchmark

Government's share of GNP s	0.4
Labour income tax rate τ_L	0.4
Capital income tax rate τ_k	0.4
Fraction of public budget allocated to investment Δ	0.1

These parameters are again chosen to mimic the Polish economy. Government's share of GNP in Poland is in the neighbourhood of 40 per cent. Estimates for capital income tax rates often differ widely. We therefore take government's share of GNP and call that number the labour tax rate and also the capital income tax rate. This procedure is similar to that adopted in Lucas (1990) and Stokey and Rebelo (1995). Finally, the fraction of GNP allocated to public investment here is

(0.4)×(0.1) or 4 per cent. This may be a bit high for Poland; it is also a bit high for Western economies, such as, for instance, the US. Nevertheless, we use this as a benchmark.

The first policy experiment we conduct is to vary government's share of GNP, holding the ratio of capital and labour tax rates constant and holding the composition of the government budget constant as well. The results are displayed in Figure 6.1. When government's share of GNP is held at 40 per cent, the growth rate of GNP in the initial period is about 7.7 per cent. This is close to the observed growth rate in the first two years of the recovery in Poland. Changing government's share of GNP has sizeable level effects. If the government share were reduced from 40 to 30 per cent, the level of GNP in period 10 would rise by 4.3 per cent, in period 20 by 4.4 per cent, in period 30 by 4.2 per cent, in period 40 by 4.2 per cent, and in period 50 by 4.3 per cent. In fact, the steady-state level of GNP is by 4.1 per cent higher with the smaller government. Cutting the government's fraction of GNP to 20 per cent has even bigger level effects on income.

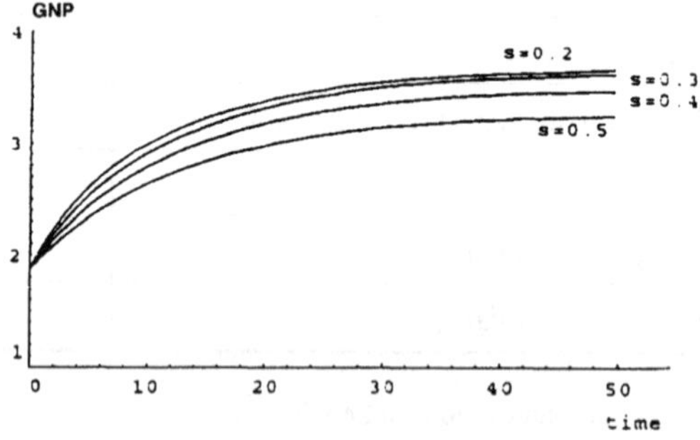

Figure 6.1 The effect of government size on capital accumulation ($\theta = 0.1$)

The qualitative results along the transition path are similar to the analytic results from Propositions 1-3 and the intuition from these propositions carries over to the results for the transitions.

In terms of growth rates, differences across the policies are large initially. In the first period, the growth rate is 7.7 per cent when government's share of GNP is 40 per cent, but when government's share of GNP is only 20 per cent, this initial growth rate is 10.6 per cent. These growth rate differentials are not monotonic over time. The growth rate between period 19 and period 20 is 0.85 per cent when $s = 0.4$, but only 0.76 per cent when $s = 0.2$.

The next experiment we perform is to change the composition of the government budget. We begin with the benchmark case of

$s = \tau_L = \tau_k = 0.4$. We vary the fraction of the government budget allocated to investment from 5 per cent over 10 per cent to 15 per cent. The results are illustrated in Figure 6.2. Raising Δ from 5 to 10 per cent raises output in period 10 by 5.7 per cent, in period 20 by 9.2 per cent, in period 30 by 10.9 per cent, in period 40 by 12 per cent, and in period 50 by 12.2 per cent. The steady-state difference in levels of GNP for these two policies is 13 per cent.

These results make sense. By increasing the fraction of public revenue allocated to infrastructure, the government can increase the speed at which the economy moves toward the steady-state. Therefore, if the government is concerned primarily with achieving high growth and only secondarily about other welfare issues, it could achieve this goal by investing heavily in infrastructure first and carrying out redistribution policies later. Perhaps this is consistent with US policy after World War II. Investment in public infrastructure was large in the 1950s and 1960s. This is, for example, when the Interstate Highway system was began. In the 1980s and 1990s public investment in infrastructure has been smaller and transfer payments larger.

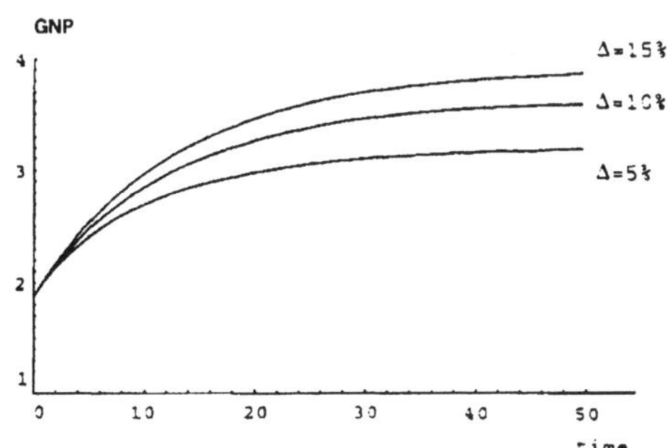

Figure 6.2 The effect of the composition of the government budget on capital accumulation ($\theta = 0.1$)

Finally, we keep the overall government size s and the composition of the government budget Δ fixed but vary the two income tax rates. When the capital income tax is lowered, we raise the labour income tax in order to keep $s = (1-\alpha)\tau_L + \alpha\tau_k$ constant. The theory predicts that raising the capital income tax in this manner lowers the steady-state level of income, but also the growth rate along the transition.

Suppose we start with $s = \tau_L = \tau_k = 0.4$ and then raise the capital tax rate to $\tau_k = 0.6$ and lower the labour tax rate to $\tau_L = 0.3$. Then the differences in levels of income after 10, 20, 30 and 40 periods are, respectively 17.7, 22.8, 24.9 and 24.9 per cent (Figure 6.3). In the steady-state the differences in income across the two policies are 26.8 per cent.

In all of the above experiments we have assumed that the output elasticity of public capital is 0.1. This value falls roughly in the middle of the estimated values of θ. Next we repeat the previous policy experiments with a smaller value θ, namely 0.05.

When the output elasticity with respect to public capital is smaller, we expect the effects of public policy changes on capital accumulation and output growth to be smaller as well.

In Figure 6.4, we change the size of the government relative to the rest of the economy, keeping fixed the ratio of the two tax rates and the composition of the government budget Δ. As *s* decreases from 40 to 30 per cent, the level of income in the steady-state rises by 6.1 per cent. This percentage change is considerably larger than in the economy with a more productive public capital'.

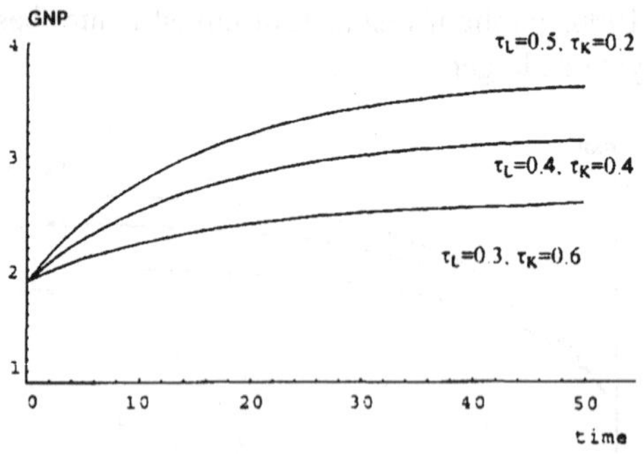

Figure 6.3 The effect of the tax rate on capital accumulation ($\theta = 0.1$)

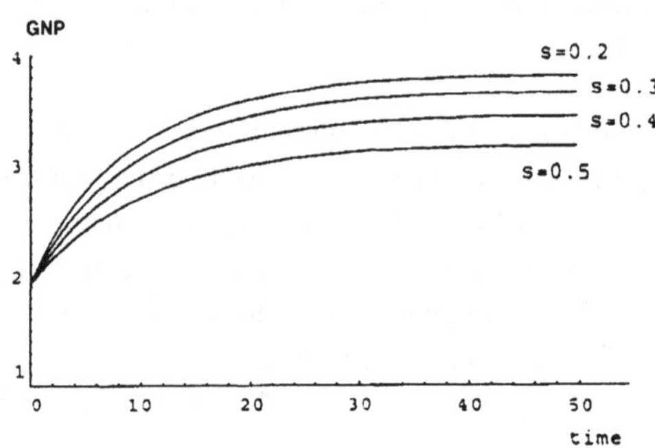

Figure 6.4 The effect of government size on capital accumulation ($\theta = 0.05$)

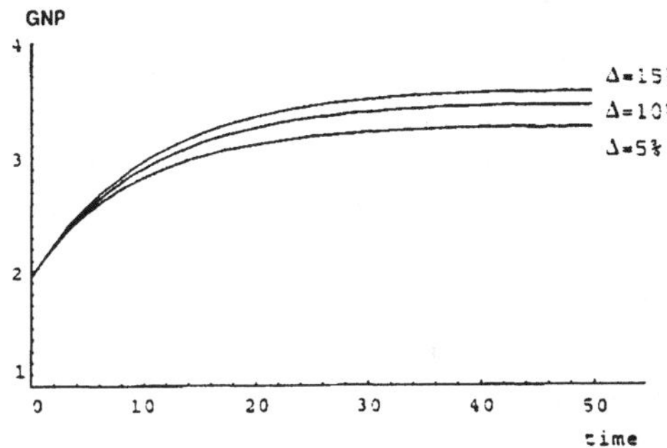

Figure 6.5 The effect of the composition of the government budget on capital accumulation (θ = 0.05)

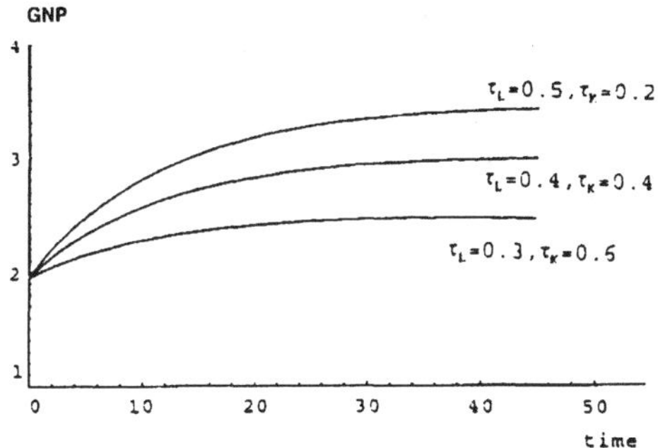

Figure 6.6 The effect of the tax rate on capital accumulation (θ = 0.05)

In Figure 6.5 we raise the fraction of the government budget allocated to investment purposes. As is evident from Figure 6.5, the effect of changing the composition of the government budget is much smaller when the output elasticity of public capital is smaller. Still, the effects are sizeable: when the fraction of the government budget allocated to investment Δ rises from 5 to 15 per cent, the steady-state level of income rises by 9.3 per cent. This finding is consistent with the earlier proposition. We would also expect to see quicker convergence to the steady-state since both capital stocks accumulate at a faster rate.

In Figure 6.6, we show how capital accumulation depends upon the factor tax rates. Again the effects on capital accumulation are large: when the labour tax rate drops from 50 to 30 per cent and the capital tax goes up from 20 to 60 per cent so that government's share of GNP remains constant, steady-state level of income falls by 45 per cent.

6.5 Concluding remarks

In this chapter we have studied how fiscal policy influences capital accumulation along the transition to the steady-state. We have used a very simple version of the Cass-Koopmans economy for this purpose. Our findings can be summarized as follows: *modest changes in fiscal policy have sizeable effects on capital accumulation.*

In this chapter we have abstracted from many issues which potentially could be very important. First, we have assumed inelastic labour supply. It turns out that when labour is supplied elastically, there are, at least for some specification of preferences, multiple steady-states. We leave the analysis of capital accumulation under various fiscal policies in this case for future work. Secondly, we have assumed that there is no international trade. The model we used was of a closed economy. It would be interesting to study these issues in an open economy under various assumptions of capital (im)mobility. Thirdly, the public capital stock in our model is a pure public good. How our findings change when this capital stock is an impure public good subject to congestion, for example, is left for future research.

References

Ai, C. and S.P. Cassou (1993) The Cumulative Benefit of Government Capital Investment. Manuscript.

Barro, R.J. (1990) Government Spending in a Simple Model of Endogenous Growth. *Journal of Political Economy*, **98**, S103-S125.

Barro, R.J. (1993) *Macroeconomics*. New York: Wiley & Sons.

Evans, P. and G. Karras (1994) Are Government Activities Productive? Evidence from a Panel of U.S. States. *Review of Economics and Statistics*, **76**, 1-11.

Fernald, J. (1996) Roads to Prosperity? Distinguishing Reality and Illusion with a Panel of U.S. Industries. Manuscript.

Finn, M. (1994) Is All Government Capital Productive? *Federal Reserve Bank of Richmond Quarterly Review*.

Fischer, S., R. Sahay, and C.A. Végh (1996) Stabilization and Growth in Transition Economies: The Early Experience. *Journal of Economic Perspectives*, **10**, 45-66.

Glomm, G. and B. Ravikumar (1994) Public Investment in Infrastructure in a Simple Growth Model. *Journal of Economic Dynamics and Control*, **18**, 1173-88.

Holtz-Eakin, D. (1994) Public-Sector Capital and the Productivity Puzzle. *Review of Economics and Statistics*, **76**, 12-21.

Hulten, C. and R.M. Schwab (1991) Public Capital Formation and the Growth of Regional Manufacturing Industries. *National Tax Journal*, 123-34.

Jones, L.E., R. Manuelli, and P. Rossi (1993) Optimal Taxation in Models of Endogenous Growth. *Journal of Political Economy*, **101**, 485-517.

King, R.G. and S. Rebelo (1990) Public Policy and Economic Growth: Developing Neoclassical Implications. *Journal of Political Economy*, **98**, 5, S127-S150.

Lucas, R.E., Jr. (1990) Supply-Side Economics: An Analytical Review. *Oxford Economic Chapters*, **42**, 293-316.

Lynde, C. and J. Richmond (1993a) Public Capital and Total Factor Productivity. *International Economic Review*, 401-44.

Lynde, C. and J. Richmond (1993b) Public Capital and Long-Run Costs in U.K. Manufacturing. *The Economic Journal*, **103**, 880-93.

Nadiri, M.I. and T.P. Mamuneas 1(994) The Effects of Public Infrastructure and R&D Capital on the Cost Structure and Performance of U.S. Manufacturing Industries. *Review of Economics and Statistics*, **76**, 22-37.

Stokey, N.L. and S. Rebelo (1995) The Growth Effects of Flat-Rate Taxes. *Journal of Political Economy*, **103**, 519-50.

Chapter 7

Knowledge Management and the Strategies of Global Business Education: From Knowledge to Wisdom

Milan Zeleny

The chapter emphasizes the role of knowledge and social infrastructure in the development of nations. It starts with the critique of the Lisbon strategy, in view of the fact that this strategy concentrates on wrong goals and relies on declarations and exhortations rather than on doing. Then, discussion turns to some World Bank studies implying that prosperity of nations is closely correlated with reliance on human and social capital. Finally, the notion and taxonomy of knowledge is discussed along with the emergence of strategic wisdom project, measurement of knowledge via added value and the institution of entrepreneurial university as main strategic concepts for achieving competitive success in the global economy.

7.1 Introduction

Knowledge and education are becoming major competitive prerequisites for economic growth. The examples of Indo-China (the China-India economic alliance), but also of USA, Japan, Taiwan and Singapore, are more than compelling. So are the successful efforts of the small states of Europe, especially Denmark, Finland, Ireland, Iceland and Luxembourg, but also Slovenia and Estonia.

Europe as a whole, that is the EU, however, is continuing to lag behind and not participating fully in the new global economy, but increasingly wrapping itself up within itself, concentrating on its endless political fights and power shifts, or finding its identity.

One of the main symptoms of this malaise was the ill-fated *Lisbon strategy* (LS). This was a typical example of how *not* to proceed in the global era. LS was formulated by the bureaucrats, engaging insufficiently in the business and entrepreneurial spheres, and not at all in the educational sphere. One cannot pull up through a pure political will, without engaging the doers.[1]

LS was not really a strategy, but a huge and very expensive pile of papers and bureaucratic exhortations. Here we can list only a few of its remarkable shortcomings and failures:

1. Its primary goal (to catch up and surpass the USA) is ill-conceived. The US is not to be competed with, but to be complemented and expanded in mutual cooperation and alliance. The undeclared strategy of Indo-China is much more powerful and represents a much bigger threat to European economic well-being. Such a misreading of global trends is remarkable.
2. Strategy is *not* about what you say, but about what you do. A laundry list of printed wishes, proclamations and declarations is not a strategy. One cannot let bureaucrats to formulate visions to be carried out by business. Business must formulate visions to be supported by politicians. The shortcomings in strategic thinking are surprising.
3. EU is primarily a political agglomeration and therefore is destined to suffer from the political ups and downs of unstable party systems. To become competitive, EU would have to abandon its bureaucratic model and transform itself into a tripartite model of Education-Business-Public Interest.
4. The notion of knowledge was misunderstood in LS: it became confused with information. Information is not knowledge. One cannot build a competitive advantage on information, which has become a globally accessible commodity.
5. Because of this confusion, the educational system did not transform itself. Instead of supplying more knowledge it strengthened its role in transferring more information. More and more graduates are therefore more and more informed, less and less knowledgeable, and certainly not wise.

It is these final two points that we shall address in this short contribution. The other points could be more important at the moment, but the last two are more deeply rooted and less easily fixed or repaired.

Also, business education is steadily becoming global and it will never again become local, regional or provincial. Not even in Europe. Management systems have globally witnessed a cumulative progression

---

[1] The EU conference, 4-5 May *In Search of New Europe* 2006 in Prague, has addressed the issues of the triune <Education-Business-Public Interest> cooperation and competitive synergy.

from *data* processing, through *information* technology, to the current *knowledge* management. *The next step is wisdom.*[2]

Corporations can be *informed*, they can be *knowledgeable*, but in the global era they must increasingly become *wise*. *Wisdom of enterprise*, its definition, taxonomy, achievement and use, are the purposes of the *wisdom project*.

Although the term *wisdom* is ancient and laden with substantial and significant philosophical meanings, our aim here is not scientific or philosophical, but *pragmatic*, *practical* and *useful*. Wisdom should become - like knowledge and information - a manageable resource for the *Corporate spine* of **4Es**: Efficiency, Effectiveness, Explicability and Ethics.

That is the strategic spine that should also dominate EU business education. Clearly, Efficiency is about doing things right, Effectiveness about doing the right things, Explicability about being able to understand and explain one's actions, and Ethics about assuming responsibility for one's actions. In the end, it is all about deciding, doing, and acting. It does not matter what we say, the only thing that matters is what we do.

7.2 Knowledge and the prosperity of nations

It can be demonstrated that the prosperous and richest nations are those well equipped in knowledge and human capital, while the poorest countries have and rely only on their natural resources and labor. Man-made, built capital is quite useless without knowledge. Bags of money cannot become productive capital without knowledge. Countries and cultures can be resource-rich, even information-rich, and yet remain knowledge-poor.

Knowledge, defined as the ability to coordinate one's actions, either alone or in cooperation with others, effectively and purposefully, is embedded within and activated by human, social and cultural institutions.

Learning to coordinate one's actions, i.e., producing, maintaining and sustaining human capital, can only take place within a requisite social infrastructure: cultural and educational institutions, family-based kinship systems and shared experiences of history, habits, values, beliefs and aspirations.

A functioning democracy is based on respect and free-market behaviour is based on trust. This is why democracy and markets are to a large extent

---

[2] "Wisdom systems" is a new working term representing a new concept, the next stage of evolution after KM (Knowledge Management), the term coined in 1987 (Zeleny, 1987).

[often hard] learned behaviours, brought forth by strong cultures and social infrastructures. Without the learned and deeply habituated respect and trust, both democracy and markets become merely gaudy, often cruel, caricatures of themselves.

Only socially and culturally strong nations - rich in human capital, family values, respect and trust can ever become prosperous - regardless of their natural, physical or financial endowments. Only the learning nations, continually and reliably evolving their human and social capital, can ever experience truly sustainable prosperity.

A wealthy nation, like a wealthy farmer, must be able to continue increasing its stock of capital. Such accumulation of the capital stock enlarges the set of alternatives and opportunities for subsequent generations, thus making current wealth sustainable.

Increased wealth also helps to generate higher income, although higher income can also be temporarily created through decreasing one's wealth and reducing the capital.

Only poor countries, like poor individuals, live mostly from their income while only maintaining or even dipping into its capital stock. Income based up on the depletion of capital is not sustainable and should not be accepted as income, but only as a consumption of capital. Only the poorest of the poor consume their own substance: they eat up their own capital endowments.

It is therefore the charge and challenge of current generations to leave future generations with more capital per capita.

There are at least four basic forms of capital:

1. *Man-made capital*, produced physical assets of infrastructures, technologies, buildings and means of transportation. This is the manufactured hardware of nations. This national hardware must be continually maintained, renewed and modernized to assure its continued productivity, efficiency and effectiveness.
2. *Natural capital*, i.e., nature-produced, renewed and reproduced "inputs" of land, water, air, raw materials, biomass and organisms. Natural capital is subject to both renewable and non-renewable depletion, degradation, cultivation, recycling and reuse.
3. *Human capital* (or human resources) refers to the continued investment in people's skills, knowledge, education, health and nutrition, abilities, motivation and effort. This is the software and brainware of a nation, perhaps the most important form of capital for rapidly developing nations.
4. *Social capital* is the enabling infrastructure of institutions, civic communities, cultural and national cohesion, collective and family

values, trust, traditions, respect and the sense of belonging. This is the voluntary, spontaneous social order which cannot be engineered, but its self-production (autopoiesis) can be nurtured, supported and cultivated.

All four of the above ***forms of*** capital must be developed in balanced, harmonious ways. The last two forms are currently the most significant and effective in terms of the creation wealth and prosperity. The vector or *portfolio of capitals*, its structure and profile, is more significant than its overall aggregate sum. A country that has all or most of its wealth in natural resources might become an international supplier, but it will not necessarily progress per se. Although the trade-offs between the capitals are often necessary, and sometimes wise and strategically desirable, they are rarely sustainable. The *optimal capital portfolio* could be negatively affected by irreversible or too frequent tradeoffs and substitutions.

In the long run, it appears to be social capital which provides the necessary supportive infrastructure for human capital to manifest itself effectively. Through renewing primarily both social and human capital, and consequently also man-made and natural capitals, the set of opportunities is being widened for future generations.

Social capital is clearly critical, although one of the most neglected and ignored. It defines people's abilities to work towards common goals and objectives in groups and organizations, form new associations and cooperative networks, and dismantle and slough off the old institutions without either conflict or violence. It is the enabling environment for human capital to become effective.

Social capital includes not only business, but also voluntary and not-for-profit associations, educational institutions, clubs, unions, media, charities and churches. A strong civic community is characterized by a preponderance of horizontal organizations, self-reliance, self-organization and self-management. On the other hand, autocratic, centralized and hierarchically vertical organizations are found in societies characterized by lower levels of trust, lower spontaneous sociability and thus of lower economic performance. The state then has to compensate for the lack of reciprocity, moral obligation, duty toward the community, and trust – a role for which the state is the least equipped and the least reliable to undertake.

Strong cultures, strong spontaneous social orders, and strong levels of civic trust tend to produce higher economic performance and generate wealth, rather than the other way around. This was powerfully shown, especially by Fukuyama (1995). Strong economic performance and wealth creation are not precursors or prerequisites to strong civil societies.

Nations with weak cultural and civic traditions will generally be poorer, saddled with strong governments, relying crucially on their natural resources and man-made capital, and neglecting the social and human spheres of existence. Wealthier and high-performing economies will typically be engendered by nations characterized by strong, dense and horizontally structured cultures of trust, cooperation and voluntary associations.

One would therefore expect the wealthiest nations to have most of their wealth embodied in social and human capital, only a lesser part in man-made or natural capital. This conclusion is supported by the studies of Serageldin (1995) at the World Bank. The following data are a few illustrative examples extracted from these studies. For example, the wealthiest and highest income countries have, on average, only 16 per cent of their total wealth in produced assets and 17 per cent in natural capital, but some 67 per cent in human resources.

It should be noted that the purpose here is not to rank or compare countries, but to emphasize the need for investing in human/social capital in order to realize long-term, sustained economic wealth. The reliance on natural resources only has brought many countries to stagnation and decline.

The poorest countries are raw material exporters, having 20 per cent of their wealth in produced assets, but 44 per cent in natural capital and a meager 36 per cent in human resources.

If we look at *a portfolio of indicators* of the US dollar wealth per capita and the percentages lodged in human/social, man-made and natural capital respectively and *in that order*, we find, for example, the following wealthy portfolio profiles:

Italy	($373,000;	82,	15,	3)
Belgium	($384,000;	83,	16,	2)
Netherlands	($379,000;	80,	18,	2)
Japan	($565,000;	81,	18,	2)
Switzerland	($647,000;	78,	19,	3)
Luxembourg	($658,000;	83,	12,	4).

Japan has virtually no natural resources. The accumulated wealth is mostly due to human and social capital investments. These can be compared with some selected "poor" country's portfolios:

Ethiopia	($1,400;	40,	21,	39)
Sierra Leone	($2, 900;	4,	18,	78)
Bhutan	($6,500;	8,	7,	85)
Zambia	($13,000;	9,	18,	73).

The above capital portfolios have so little investment in human and social capital that their future prospects are quite discouraging. On the other hand, there are some poor and developing countries which seem to have the right "mix" of capitals, indicating a possible economic takeoff in the future:

Viet Nam	($2,600;	74,	15,	11)
Slovakia	($33,000;	78,	17,	5)
Czech Republic	($50,000;	66,	15,	19)
Mexico	($74,000;	73,	11,	16)
Slovenia	($111,000;	67,	16,	17).

Richer countries are generally those which invest more in their human capital, education, nutrition, health care, etc., over longer periods of time.

Some poor countries have relatively high incomes because they do not invest enough in renewing their capital portfolio, but actually consume their capital (essentially consuming their next-year plant seed). In particular, Sub-Saharan countries have recently registered very high levels of disinvestment, negative savings and capital depletion. The countries of Eastern Europe (most of them, without significant exceptions) are artificially increasing their current incomes for political reasons, but at the cost of depleting their long-term wealth. Without attempting any fashionable and often meaningless comparisons, it is quite discouraging to see many of these potentially promising countries rapidly disinvesting their educational, health care, nutritional and cultural endowments, slipping into corruption and the 'anything-goes' culture, remaining still culturally blind to dirty money and fashionably myopic about their future.

In many such countries, the sheer number of students has skyrocketed, yet the quality, employability and global impact of their quantitative educational institutions has declined. The budget allocation criterion for state-funded institutions should not be the number of accepted students, or even the number of graduated students, but the number of graduates gainfully employed within a year after graduation. These are all very obvious conclusions, but only now are qualitative educational reforms being contemplated.

Many World Bank studies (for example, Serageldin, 1995) have confirmed the leading role of human capital in economic development. With the exception of some raw material exporters, human capital exceeds both natural capital and produced assets combined: sustainable development is best achieved by investing in people. Yet the bulk of current economic policies remains focused on man-made capital, i.e. on less than one-fifth of total wealth formation. In spite of Serageldin's studies, even the World Bank and similar institutions have emphasized building assorted Aswan dams rather than founding technology institutes and entrepreneurial universities, educating people and expanding their self-reliance and self-managing opportunities and abilities. That is why most of the world still remains poor and poverty is on the rise after some 50 years of misplaced efforts.

Additional arguments along these lines, emphasizing software over hardware, institutions over dams, and knowledge over information, can be found in Stiglitz (1999) and in his World Bank studies on the Knowledge Economy.

Many of the misguided policies are the result of naive beliefs and neo-pagan market worshipping, particularly in Russia and the countries of Eastern Europe. Free-market efficiency is only one of the many by-products of pre-existing moral communities. One cannot prefer investing in hardware just because it is easier, measurable, and thus more prone to corruption.

Without moral communities, the unfettered free market is neither conservative nor constructive but a most radically disruptive force, relentlessly dissolving the loyalty of corporations to their communities, customers to their neighborhood merchants, athletes to their teams and nations, teams to their cities, and so on. Without the culturally preformed, spontaneous social orders of trust, loyalty and reciprocity, a nation cannot achieve and maintain sustainable wealth.

It is therefore necessary to turn our attention to *knowledge*.

7.3 Taxonomy of knowledge

What is knowledge?

Knowledge is the purposeful coordination of action. Achieving its purpose is its sole proof or demonstration. Its quality can be judged from the quality of the attainment (its product) or even from the quality of the coordination (its process).

What is meant when we say that somebody knows or possesses knowledge? We imply that we expect one to be capable of coordinated action towards some goals and objectives. Coordinated action is the test of possessing knowledge. *All doing is knowing, and all knowing is doing.*

Every act of knowing brings forth a world. We bring forth a hypothesis about the relationships and test it through action; if we succeed in reaching our goal - we know.

Bringing forth a world of coordinated action is human knowledge.

Bringing forth a world manifests itself in all our action and all our being. Knowing is effective (i.e., coordinated and successful) action. So, knowledge is *not* information. *Everybody in the world is now informed, only some are knowledgeable, just a few are wise.*

Our concern, clearly, is the last row of Table 7.1: ***the wisdom row***. While information allows us to do things right (efficiency), knowledge already aspires to also do the right things (effectiveness). Doing the right thing, especially in business, requires not only knowing how, but also knowing why. *Explicability* of purpose is an essential ingredient of its effectiveness in attainment. *Wisdom is about explicability and ethics* of our doing.

Table 7.1 Taxonomy of knowledge

	Technology	**Analogy (baking bread)**	**Effect**	**Purpose (Metaphor)**
Data	EDP	Elements: H_2O, yeast, bacteria, starch molecules	Muddling through	Know-Nothing
Information	MIS	Ingredients: flour, water, sugar, spices + recipe	Efficiency	Know-What
Knowledge	DSS, ES, AI	Coordination of the baking process → result, product	Effectiveness	Know-How
Wisdom	WS, MSS	Why bread? Why this way?	Explicability	Know-Why

Many informed people know what to do, quite a few knowledgeable experts know how to do it, but only a few *wise persons* know why it should (or should not) be done. Wisdom project is of importance to all countries.

7.4 Wisdom Project – expected effects and impacts

- *Sapientia et doctrina* (the motto of my university) should receive real, institutional and global embodiment
- EU schools should differentiate themselves through wisdom focus - a powerful recognition attribute, eminently suitable for the global era
- Students and teachers, through all courses and projects, should pursue wisdom: asking Why, expanding inquiry, and embedding strategic thinking throughout all individual and institutional learning activities
- Any school can aspire to become an Institution of Inquiry, the Why? university, demonstrating its wisdom search embodied within its culture

- New courses shall emerge and existing courses will be revitalized by the added dimension, completing the chain of data-information-knowledge-wisdom
- EU schools should assume leadership worldwide in defining, teaching, applying and practicing the wisdom concept, taking it from the realm of philosophy into the realm of human action
- Because ethics and ethical behavior emerges naturally in response to inquiry, to asking Why?, EU should assume leadership in evolving ethics as an integral part of our teaching and doing, not as an imported partial focus or dimension
- Wisdom is a powerful cross-cultural, cross-generational and universally revered concept and EU should assume a leading role in the emerging East-West dialogue
- Business schools should derive pragmatic benefits and reputation from the active pursuit of concepts like wisdom corporation, inquiring systems, wisdom management, wisdom support systems, and strategy as an attainment of corporate wisdom
- Strategy, strategic thinking and strategic inquiry should become permanent rather than project-oriented characteristics of business curricula, allowing innovation spirit penetrate throughout the institution.

7.5 Wisdom: on the art of asking why

Wisdom is *knowing why* things should or should not be done - locally, regionally and globally - and is, and will remain, in short supply. Wisdom is not practiced purposefully and it is not taught in schools.

Asking Why is fundamentally different from asking *How*.

Whenever we explore a coordinated process in the sense of *What* or *How* (What is to be done, how sequenced, how performed, etc.) we already accept that process. The process is becoming *a given*, subject to learning or mastering, but not subject to exploration or change.

It is only when we start asking *Why* (Why do it at all, why this operation and not another, why this sequence, etc.) that we question the very structure of knowledge (coordination of action) and introduce the possibility of change. The *Whys* and the *Why Nots* are the most important questions in business and management and they should not be taken as given.

In the global economy, frequent or continuous strategic change will become the norm of competitiveness. Doing the same, given thing better and better (continuous improvement) will be inadequate for strategic success. One has to *do things differently* (not just better) and *do different things*, not just the same ones. Such an important mode of strategic thinking cannot be learned and mastered by asking *How*, but mainly by asking *Why*.

7.6 Strategy and strategic action

All presented concepts of the spine of the **4Es** and the taxonomy of knowledge have one important thing in common: they are all about *action*, all about *doing*.

Only information is always and only about descriptions. *Information is a symbolic description of action*, past, present or future. Yet business is not about managing descriptions, but about managing action. So, the need to move from information to knowledge and wisdom is tantamount to moving from words to deeds.

Wisdom project would usher in a new era of global corporate strategy. Strategy also is not about statements, but about action. Traditionally, organization executives prepare a set of statements, descriptions of future action: mission, vision, set of goals, plan or pattern for action and similar artifacts. All such statements are information. It all remains to be translated into action, into corporate knowledge.

Strategy is about what we do, not about what we say we do or desire to do. Strategy is about action, not about the description of action. Strategy is about doing, not about talking about it.

Your strategy is what you are doing. And what you are doing is your strategy.

All the rest is just words.

Because all organizations do something, all organizations already have a strategy. Their executives should stop managing information by issuing statements and start managing knowledge by coordinating action.

Let us at least outline the steps and proper sequencing of the strategic process:

First, we have to create a detailed map of key corporate activities to find out what the company is doing - to reveal its actual strategy that is embedded in action. Remarkably, many corporations do not know their own processes, what they are doing; in other words, do not know their own strategy. They only know what they say, through their mission statements.

Secondly, after creating the coherent activity map, one has to analyse the activities by comparing them to the benchmarks of competitors, industry standards or stated aspirations.

Thirdly, so-called value-curve maps are produced in order to differentiate one's activities from those of the competition.

Differentiation, not catching up or imitation, is the key to effective competitiveness and strategy.

Fourthly, identified selected activities are changed - in order to fill the opportunity spaces revealed by value-curve maps - as being most effective for successful differentiation. The rest of action space is conserved.

Fifnally, after a newly changed action space (and its activity map) has emerged and become reliably functional, the descriptive mission and vision statement can be drawn for the purposes of communication. The description now actually describes the action and the action reflects the description.

7.7 Wisdom and ethics

Wisdom and ethics are clearly closely related, often being indistinguishable and inseparable. An unethical person cannot be considered wise. Both concepts are related to strategy and strategic action.

Also ethics, in this context, is about action, rather than doing.

The most remarkable lapses in ethical behaviour have occurred in companies with admirable ethical rules and covenants, impressive and ethical vision statements and other elaborate props that simulate and substitute for ethical know-how. Enron's walls were covered with descriptions and statements on ethics. The problem with corporate ethics is not with knowing what is right, but with doing right and being good.

Truly ethical behaviour does not come from deliberate judgment, decision making, reasoning and learning the rules, but from human coping with immediate circumstances, from *being and acting good,* not just describing what good means, out of context and devoid of action.

It is clear that teaching ethics, i.e., providing descriptions, does not necessarily lead to ethical behavior and deeds, to being good and wise.

There is a difference between reading or learning an ethical rule, and putting it into action consciously and purposefully, or acting ethically through mastering one's microcontext, i.e., *acting ethically* through one's own internal self-interest. In order to be truly ethical, one cannot be consciously and intentionally "ethical."

7.8 All about adding value

Knowledge is measured by the value our coordination of effort, action and process adds to materials, technology, energy, services, information, time and other inputs used or consumed in the process. *Knowledge is measured by added value.*

In any business (and human) transaction, value has to be *added to both* participating sides: the provider *and* the customer. Adding value is what makes the transaction satisfactory and sustainable.

There are two kinds of value to be created: *value for the business* and *value for the customer.* Both parties must benefit: the business - in order to make it; the customer - in order to buy it. In the global age it is precisely this business-customer *value competition* that is emerging as the hardest and the busiest battleground.

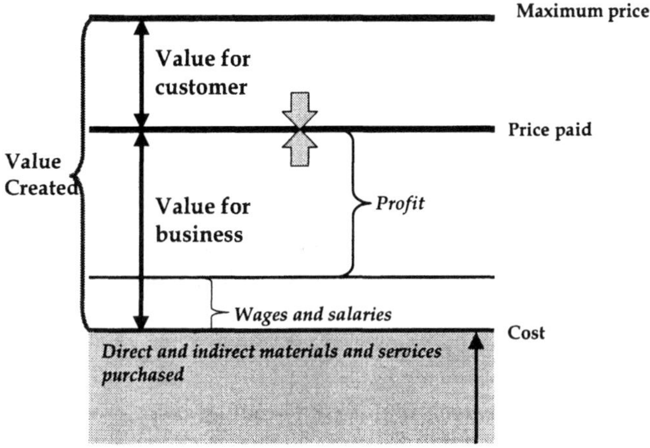

Figure 7.1 Adding value for the customer

In Figure 7.1 we attempt to explain the process of creating new value. This is crucial for the identification and assessment of innovation.

First, the customer pays for the service or product: the *price paid.* The producer subtracts the *cost incurred*, including all direct and indirect materials and services purchased. The difference is the *added value* for the business. This added value can also be interpreted as the *value of knowledge* engaged in producing the service or product. In order to pay wages and salaries, the production process and its coordination must generate this added value. Added value is the only source of corporate wages and salaries and profits.

If the added value does not *cover* the wages and salaries, then these must be correspondingly lowered. If no value has been added, then the value of knowledge is zero and no payment can be attributed to it. The business must add enough value in order to *cover* at least its workers and managers, their salaries and wages. If even more value has been created, then *profits* can be realized, up to the price received.

The customer, of course, must be willing and ready to pay more for the service/product than he actually paid. The *maximum price* the customer would be willing to pay must exceed the price the producer has asked for. The difference is the added *value for customer*.

If there is no value for customer - the maximum price is lower than the price to be paid - then the customer would not buy the service or product.[3] In a competitive market, the customer pays money only for the value received, i.e. the value for the customer.

7.9 The Entrepreneurial University

We are entering an era of reassessment of business programs, shifting from the description of action (functional, scientific model) towards action itself, i.e. an *entrepreneurial model*.

It is being realized globally that business is a *profession* and business schools are *professional schools*, comparable schools of medicine or law. Professions are always more about knowledge and wisdom, less about information, always more about doing and less about describing.

It is challenging to contemplate why business schools model themselves more on physics, chemistry and economics and less on medicine and law.

Business *IS* a profession.

Professions work with an accepted body of knowledge (not information), certify and guarantee acceptable practice, are *committed to the public good*, and rely on an enforceable *code of ethics*.

Professions integrate knowledge and practice in a wise and ethical way, serving the public, focusing on clients' needs.

Education in business must involve history, moral reasoning, theology, logic and, most importantly - practical *knowledge, wisdom* and *ethics*.

Bennis and O'Toole (2005) recently wrote: *The problem is not that business schools have embraced scientific rigor but that they have forsaken other forms of knowledge.*

Every business school should run its own business, as proposed by Polaroid's E. Land. This need for practice, innovation and entrepreneurship takes us to the notion of the *entrepreneurial university*.

The entrepreneurial university not only produces knowledge (rather than information) but engages in a new mission of *capitalization of knowledge*. It produces not only graduates and alumni, but also firms and companies: it becomes an economic actor in the regional and possibly - through a network - also in global economic and social development. This

[3] Unless *forced to* by circumstances of monopoly or the lack of alternative choices.

new mission puts the university into direct cooperation with the state and corporate sectors, forming the *triad of cooperation*.

From the original conservatory of information and knowledge, through the producer and transmitter of information and knowledge, to the *university as an entrepreneur* - that is the vision in which the triune EU network of alliances would be preeminently and prominently *positioned* to assume global leadership in translating into reality.

The university-industry-government is the proper triad for successful regional development. *New firms and their capitalization* is the proper output of a professional, entrepreneurial school. One-way, linear outflow without feedback is replaced by a self-sustaining cycle of knowledge and wisdom.

The entrepreneurial university still produces graduates and publications, of course, but packages them in firms and companies to take the created knowledge out with the newly minted entrepreneurs.

The trend is towards global alliances and networks in business and economic cooperation. It is moving away from self-absorbed islands of bureaucracy and political roller-coasters. Education, entrepreneurship and innovation are the next frontiers, even for Europe.

References

Bennis, W. G. and J. O'Toole (2005) How Business Schools Lost Their Way. *Harvard Business Review*, May, 1-9.

Etzkowitz, H. (2004) The Evolution of the Entrepreneurial University. *International Journal Technology and Globalisation*, **1**(1), 64-77.

Fukuyama, F. (1995) *Trust: The Social Virtues and the Creation of Prosperity*. New York: Free Press.

Serageldin, I. (1995) Sustainability and the Wealth of Nations: First Steps in an Ongoing Journey. *Third Annual World Bank Conference on Environmentally Sustainable Development*, Washington, DC September 30.

Serageldin, I. (1995) Monitoring Environmental Progress: A Report on Work in Progress. *Environmentally Sustainable Development Series. Washington, DC:* The World Bank.

Stiglitz, J.E. (1999) *Public Policy for a Knowledge Economy*. London: The World Bank Department for Trade and Industry, Center for Economic Policy Research.

Zeleny, M. (1987) Management Support Systems: Towards Integrated Knowledge Management. *Human Systems Management*, **7**(1), 59-70.

Zeleny, M. (2002) Knowledge of enterprise: knowledge management or knowledge technology? *International Journal Information Technology and Decision Making*, **1**(2), 181-207.

Zeleny, M. (2005) *Human Systems Management: Integrating Knowledge, Management and Systems*. World Scientific Publishers.

Zeleny, M. (2006) Knowledge-Information Autopoietic Cycle: Towards The Wisdom Systems. *International Journal Management and Decision Making*, **7**(1), 3-18.

Chapter 8

Modelling of the Labour Market in a Transition Economy

Mikhail Mikhalevich

Labour market in a transition economy is considered as the market with imperfect competition. A new approach, based on dynamic macromodels of interaction between monopsonic labor market and market of goods and services is developed and analyzed. Conditions of economic stabilization and emergence of economic cycles for these models are investigated. Essential aspects of employment theory for the early stages of transition are discussed.

8.1 Introduction

The current social situation in post-communist countries is certainly an extremely difficult one. Various grave problems exist: rising inequalities in income both at downward and upward stages of the business cycle are manifested through islands of prosperity in the sea of distress and poverty, as well as in capital flights and growing indebtedness. All of these factors lead to a rise in the level of crime rate in the society. Extremely low wages are the main reason of such a situation.

The industrial decline at the initial stage of reforms is not accompanied by the expected corresponding growth of unemployment, especially in countries of the former Soviet Union (see Appendix to this chapter, Tables A8.1, A8.2). As a result, productivity of labour decreases faster than real wages, which leads to an amplification of the recession. Traditional instruments of economic policy demonstrate their low efficiency in attempts to improve the wage condition, especially in countries with low unemployment and high rates of GDP decline. Therefore the theoretical investigation, which will be further applied to the mentioned countries, is necessary.

It is rather difficult to analyse the peculiarities of labour market in a transition economy through traditional means. A new methodological approach is necessary for this purpose. For instance, many phenomena, which are observed at the post-communist countries' labour markets, could be explained considering the latter as a market with imperfect competition.

Theoretical investigations of the labour market with imperfect competition started in the 1930s.

J. Robinson (1933, 1962) was one of the first economists to systematically study imperfect competition in the labour market (and in other market segments as well). Robinson analysed its influence on general economic dynamics. In her publications, she focused on microeconomic analysis of monopolism and monopsony, giving interpretation of several fundamental economic categories from the viewpoint of differences between competitive and monopsonic markets. The progress of trade unions and the establishment of state control over wages were considered the main directions of restricting the consequences of imperfect competition. Little attention was paid to the **macroeconomic** analysis of the systems with non-competitive labour markets. These problems are not yet solved, probably because of the fact that the labour market in developed countries is restricted to the standards of a competitive market. (Particular attention to such problems observed in the publications by the leftist post-Keynesians, for example, in Bortis, 1997 could be explained mainly by tradition). The interest in non-competitive waging analysis increased during the last decade as the result of post-communist studies of the economy. For instance, the peculiarities of the labour market in a transition economy were explained in Polterovich (2003) from the viewpoint of social partnership theory. It is difficult, though, to believe in such explanations given the Gini coefficient rates of growth in the post-communist countries for the last 5 years are approximately equal to the rates of increase of GDP. Another approach, using the model of a two-side monopoly competition (trade unions against employers) and is considered in Ciupagea and Turlea (1997). Papers of Aslund, Layard (1993) and Commander, Coricelli (1995) also contributed to the labour market analysis in post-communist countries. In particular, they paid a great deal of attention to the official statistical information's accuracy and analysed the factors that influenced employers' behaviour. It should be noted that several fundamental works hare appeared in recent years (Boal, 1995; Manning, 2003) in which the authors admitted that specific forms of monopsony could be also typical for the market economy. Professor A. Manning and his scientific school developed this theory; they paid a great deal of attention to the microeconomic analysis of such phenomena.

It is also true that macroeconomic research is an important part of the existing methodology of economic studies. The influence of imperfect competition on the labour market could be very important for some other market segments and economic processes in general. Different quantitative and qualitative methods, including mathematical modelling, have been applied to study this influence. In our chapter we introduce a new methodology to analyse the labour market for countries in transition.

This chapter applies dynamic macroeconomic models based on the assumption about monopoly consumption or monopsony in the labour market of a transition economy.

This assumption can be justified for the following reasons. High levels of concentration and specialization were typical for industrial enterprises in centrally planned economies, especially in machinery, mining, ferrous and color metal production. This situation was a result of technological peculiarities, but sometimes it simplified decision making in planned economy. The number of controlled indicators was reduced for specialized enterprises, thus, the development of plans for them was not very difficult and the control of their realization was more effective. This situation was preserved during the early stages of transition, but the leading managers (sometimes, owners) of the former state enterprises did not take state interests into account. They acted on the basis of their short-term goals in situations of growth of financial and social instability. Absence of strong and independent trade unions in the majority of post-socialist countries (except for Poland and, in some branches, Romania) also was the precondition for monopsony.

In our chapter, we consider the models of economic dynamics for the case of monopsonic labour market and restricted time interval of planning for employers.

The structure of the chapter is as follows. Section 8.2 considers a model of a monopoly price (wage) formation on the labour market with a monopolist-employer (the so-called monopsonic labour market). Section 8.3 analyses the relation between the wages and production dynamics and investigates the mechanisms of depression in a market economy. A more complicated model with variable prices is considered in section 8.4 to demonstrate the possibilities of appearance of specific cycles in the systems with a monopsonic labour market. Section 8.5 concludes the chapter offering some discussion of essential aspects of employment theory for the early stages of transition.

8.2 The employer's behaviour model

Let us consider a monopsonic labour market with the following structure. There are potentially employed individuals, who supply their labour, and a single monopolist, who is the consumer of labour (an employer). It is assumed that the latter is aware of the labour supply function and the value of demand for goods that are being produced using the labour acquired. The monopolist acts with respect to only his short-term interests striving to maximize his profit obtained from the production of goods. Let us also assume that his additional costs, associated with labour consumption (indirect tax on the wage fund, social payments, etc.) are proportional to the value of the total wage fund *W*.

Let us consider the function *S* (*W*) - the dependency between *W* and the maximal amount of labour that the employer can purchase given the limits of the total wage fund by changing the value of wages ω. In fact, $S(W) = \max_{\omega \in X(W)} L_s(\omega)$, where $L_s(\omega)$ is the labour supply function, $X(W) = \{\omega : \omega L_s(\omega) \leq W, \omega \geq 0\}$. Such properties of *S*(*W*) as continuity, concavity and monotony follow directly from the similar assumptions about the properties of the function $L_s(\omega)$.

Let us denote the amount of labour acquired by *T*, *U*(*T*) is the utility of labour consumption by the employer, labour cost multiplier is denoted as $H = 1 + h$, where *h* is the value of the associated costs per wage fund unit.

It should be noted that the employer always acquires the maximum amount of labour within his wage fund limit. Indeed, a lower amount implies less gross profit for the same labour cost, and such a decision will not be the best for the employer. The employer also decreases the size of the wage fund, if the restricted demand for produced goods forces the employer to cut the amount of labour acquired. Then the monopolist-employer will select the value of *W* so as to maximize the following function:

$$F(W) = U(S(W)) - W(1 + h)$$

provided that $W \geq 0$.

We can assume that the utility of labour consumption for the employer lies in the possibility of obtaining income from the sale of goods produced using this labour; therefore,

$$U(T) = min\ (lT, \alpha v),$$

where *l* is the amount of value added newly created by a unit of labour, *v* is the demand for products, and α is the portion of the added value included in the unit value of the products.

Thus, the value of *W* established by the employer will be the solution of the optimization problem

$$F(W) = \min(lS(W), \alpha v) - HW \rightarrow \max \qquad (8.1)$$

for $W \geq 0$.

The function $F(W)$ is also continuous and concave under the assumptions mentioned. The point of its maximum will be $W^* = \min(W^{(1)}, W^{(2)})$, where $W^{(1)}$ is a solution of the equation $S(W) = \frac{\alpha v}{l}$ and $W^{(2)}$ is determined from the relation $\frac{H}{l} \in \hat{\partial} S(W)$. Here $\hat{\partial} S(W)$ is the generalized (Clarke) derivative of the function $S(W)$. The point W=0 could also be the solution of the problem (8.1), but this case could be avoided if we assumed that the derivative of $L_s(\omega)$ function in zero point was sufficiently large, thus $\inf \hat{\partial} S(0) > \frac{H}{l}$.

This assumption seems quite natural for the functions of labour supply, usually applied in economic analysis such as $L(\omega) = a_1 \omega^{a_2}$ or $L(\omega) = \ln(1 + b\omega)$, where $a_1 > 0$, $0 < a_2 < 1$, $b > 0$ are parameters of the functions. Further on we will consider the case when the function $S(W)$ is differentiable. In the case of non-differentiable function, the difference will be in technical aspects, but principal conclusions will be quite the same.

It should be noted that only one of the two components, $W^{(1)}$, of the solution W^*, depends on demand v. Thus, in the case of a deep economic decline when the value of v is decreased, the wage fund is also decreased, i.e. an absolute decline of employees' level of life takes place. In the case of economic growth the wage fund will increase up to some limit defined by the point $W^{(2)}$. Further economic growth (an increase of v) will be accompanied by a constant value of the total wage fund. The relative decline (in comparison with total demand) of employees' incomes will be observed in this case. The dependence between the wage and demand will be non-linear as the result of the effects mentioned above.

The above-considered model also allows us to account for the low level of unemployment in those transition countries experiencing a deep business depression. It is advantageous for a monopolist-employer to establish the wages, so that the labour supply is equal to the labour demand. A lower price of labour will not allow the monopolist to realize fully the feasible income due to the properties of $L_s(\omega)$, and a higher price will decrease the pure utility of labour consumption due to high labour purchase cost. Thus, there will be no extra labour force (i.e., unemployment in its classical understanding) in the labour market. Redundant labour will simply be ousted from the market due to low wages. Actually, there exists some unemployment that, first, is created by employers to force the employees to agree with low monopoly wages, secondly, is formed due to disagreement between the expected (used by employer for waging) and actual values of demand, and, thirdly, appears as frictional and structural unemployment. However, even taking into account the above-mentioned factors, the total level of unemployment will still be considerably lower than the unemployment estimates obtained from the classical labour market models under the condition of a high rate of production decrease.

A further development of the suggested model will be to consider a dynamic system consisting of a linear autocorrelation equation, which connects the values of demand and the wage fund, and the previously considered equality, which determines the wage fund through demand.

8.3 The dynamic macromodel with constant prices

In the previous section, it was assumed that demand was not dependent upon wages. Actually, this is not the case. The current employees' income affects the value of their demand for consumer goods; however, the effect of consumer savings on this demand turns out to be much more significant. The components of the aggregate demand such as demand of these consumers whose income is not obtained from employment, and demand for investment and exports do not depend on the wages. Moreover, the employer, when making his decisions on the wage level, is not guided by the demand level in the current period of time (which is unknown and will depend on the decision yet to be made), but by the known value of demand in the previous period. All this requires the development of dynamic wage formation models. One of them, constructed on the basis of the model discussed in the previous section, will be considered below.

Suppose time t is discrete, with step equal to one. We will assume that the function $S(W)$ does not depend on time, is non-negative, continuous, and takes zero values for the minimum possible wage fund $W \leq W_0$ (as a special case, $W_0 = 0$ is possible). Suppose this function is concave, increasing and differentiable for $W > W_0$, and its derivative to the right of W_0 is bounded. Assume also that the coefficients l and α are independent of time. Denote by v_t the demand at a moment of time t, and by W^t the wage fund at the same moment of time. Suppose W^t is determined at each time interval on the basis of the above-considered model of monopoly price formation using v_t as the final demand. In other words, we have

$$W^t = \min(W^{(1)t},\ W^{(2)t}), \tag{8.2}$$

where $W^{(1)t} = S^{-1}\left(\frac{\alpha v_t}{l}\right)$, $W^{(2)t} = (S')^{-1}\ (Hl^{-1})$, $S^{-1}(\bullet)$ and $(S')^{-1}(\bullet)$ are functions inverse to $S(W)$ and $S'(W)$. From the assumptions made it follows that these functions exist for $W \geq W_0$, the function $S^{-1}(\bullet)$ being increasing and $(S')^{-1}(\bullet)$ decreasing. Let us redefine the function $S^{-1}(\bullet)$ by putting $S^{-1}(0)=W_0$. Note also that for $v\geq 0$ the function $g(v)=\min\left(S^{-1}\left(\frac{\alpha v}{l}\right),(S')^{-1}\left(Hl^{-1}\right)\right)$ will satisfy the Lipschitz condition for some constant L_1.

Let us consider the case where the demand is determined at each subsequent moment of time as a weighted average value of the demand at the previous moment of time and the current consumer income, i.e.,

$$v_{t+1}=(1-\rho)v_t+\rho W^t,\quad t=0,\,1,\,\ldots, \tag{8.3}$$

where $0<\rho<1$ is some weighting factor. Due to the above-mentioned reasons, the quantity ρ may be considered to be a rather small one.

We will analyze the properties of the sequence $\{v_t\}$ constructed according to (8.3). The following statement is true:

Theorem 1

Let $\rho<\frac{1}{2L}$, *where* $L=1+L_1$. *Then, the sequence* $\{v_t\}$, *which is determined according to (8.2) and (8.3), is converging, and its limit (depending on the value of* v_0*) may be either the solution of the equation*

$$S^{-1}\left(\frac{\alpha}{l}v\right)=v,$$

denoted hereafter by $v^{(1)}$, if $v^{(1)}<(S')^{-1}(Hl^{-1})$, *or the point*

$$v^{(2)}=(S')^{-1}(Hl^{-1}),$$

if $v^{(2)}\geq v^{(1)}$.

This theorem was proved in Koshlai, Mikhalevich, Sergienko (1999).

Let us now consider the disposition of the equilibrium points $v^{(1)}$ and $v^{(2)}$ and the behaviour of the convergence of the sequence $\{v_t\}$. The following cases are possible.

1. The equation $S^{-1}\left(\frac{\alpha}{l}v\right)=v$ has two roots: $\bar{v}^{(1)}$ and $\hat{v}^{(1)}$, $\bar{v}^{(1)}<\hat{v}^{(1)}$, on the interval $[0; S((S')^{-1}(Hl^{-1}))]$, with $v^{(2)}=(S')^{-1}(Hl^{-1})>\hat{v}^{(1)}$ existing (see Appendix, Figure A8.1). In particular, if $W_0=0$, then $\bar{v}^{(1)}=0$.

In Figures A8.1-3 of the Appendix, the following designations are assumed: →→→ means that v_t increases and ←←← means that v_t decreases.

The sequence $\{v_t\}$ will converge to the point $\bar{v}^{(1)}$ if v_t belongs to $[0;\ \hat{v}^{(1)})$ for some t, and to the point $v^{(2)}$ if $v_t \in (\hat{v}^{(1)}, \infty)$. In this case, if $v_t \in (\bar{v}^{(1)}, \hat{v}^{(1)})$, then a decrease in production (reduction of demand v) will be accompanied by a reduction in real wages W, which will lead to another decrease in production. When the sequence $\{v_t\}$ reaches a sufficiently small neighbourhood of the lower equilibrium point $\bar{v}^{(1)}$, the decrease in production will slow down, and, at certain moments of time, the demand may increase if $v_t < \bar{v}^{(1)}$ has been satisfied before. However, the rate of increase will be insignificant, the increase itself will be small, and the demand will be stabilized eventually at the point $\bar{v}^{(1)}$.

On the half-interval $(\bar{v}^{(1)}, v^{(2)}]$, the convergence of the sequence $\{v_t\}$ to the point of the upper equilibrium between the demand and wages $v^{(2)}$ will be accompanied by an increase in demand, but if $W^t < W^{(2)t}$, then also by an increase in wages. At a value of demand exceeding $v^{(2)}$, it will decrease, but the real wages will remain unchanged. Note that on the strength of the property of the function $(S')^{-1}(\bullet)$ a decrease in H (for example, due to reduction in tax load on the wage fund) will lead to an upward shift of the horizontal half-line $W = (S')^{-1}(Hl^{-1})$, however, in this case, the position of the curve $W - S^{-1}\left(\frac{\alpha}{l}v\right)$ will not change, and, consequently, the disposition of the points $\bar{v}^{(1)}$ and $\hat{v}^{(1)}$ will not change, neither. Thus, the above-described mechanism of economic depression on the half-interval $[\bar{v}^{(1)}, \hat{v}^{(1)})$ will remain the same. This measure may change the situation only in the case where the value of the demand belongs to the interval between the previous and the new values of $v^{(2)}$. In other cases, in order to eliminate the negative dynamics, it is necessary to shift the curve $W - S^{-1}\left(\frac{\alpha}{l}v\right)$ to the left and upward. Such an effect could be achieved either through a decrease in labour force supply in the monopolized segment of the economy (for example, due to development of small and medium sized enterprises that do not relate to this segment), or through an increase in the value-added share α (for example, by reducing the taxation of income and added value, and executing radical structural and technological transformations). However, these measures may just narrow the boundaries of the depression domain $[\bar{v}^{(1)}, \hat{v}^{(1)})$ and raise the lower limit of demand reduction $\bar{v}^{(1)}$, but they do not fully eliminate the associated negative consequences.

2. The equation $S^{-1}\left(\frac{\alpha}{l}v\right)=v$ has a unique root within the interval $[0; S((S')^{-1}(Hl^{-1}))]$ (see Appendix, Figure A8.2). The intersection point of the lines $W=v$ and $W=(S')^{-1}(Hl^{-1})$ also falls into this interval. In this case, there exists the unique point $v^{(1)}$, satisfying the conditions of Theorem 1. For a value of demand greater than $v^{(1)}$, production will decrease to the level defined by this point. In this case, the real wages remain the same if $v_t > S((S')^{-1}(Hl^{-1}))=v'$, and start to decrease as soon as the demand is less than v'. Since the amount of labour force purchased by a monopolist-employer remains the same with constant wages, and the quantity of production decreases with a fall in demand, a drop in labour capacity will occur in this case, and will continue more slowly after the reduction in the wages takes place.

A special case of the above-considered situation is when the scope and the rate of depression do not depend up on changes in the labour cost multiplier *H*. This case corresponds to the deepest and longest-occurring business depression. The only way to reduce the negative consequences of the depression will be a reduction in labour supply accompanied by a growth in production profitability. This will cause a left-ward and upward shift of the curve $W=S^{-1}\left(\frac{\alpha}{l}v\right)$ and will raise the limit $v^{(1)}$ up to which the business depression will continue.

3. For $v=v'$ the inequality $S^{-1}\left(\frac{\alpha}{l}v\right)\geq v$ is fulfilled, and there exists the point $v^{(2)}$ of intersection of the lines $W=v$ and $W=(S')^{-1}(Hl^{-1})$ lying to the right of v'. In particular, the curve $W=S^{-1}\left(\frac{\alpha}{l}v\right)$ may be tangent to the line $W=v$ (see Appendix, Figure A8.3).

In the absence of tangency points $\bar{v}$ the demand v_t will increase up to the point $v^{(2)}$ if it is less than $v^{(2)}$ for some *t* and will decrease if $v_t > v^{(2)}$. This growth can be stopped at one of the points $\bar{v}$, if any. In this case, a left-ward and upward shift of the curve $W=S^{-1}\left(\frac{\alpha}{l}v\right)$ will restore the growth. In contrast to the cases considered before, such a shift will not affect the dynamics of depression with constant wages. The depth and the rate of the depression could be lowered through a reduction of the additional cost *h* associated with the use of the labour force. Here, recommendations for overcoming the crisis will be opposite to those that were effective in the previous cases.

Thus, monopolistic price formation in the labour market may be the cause of a number of negative economic processes such as economic depression, decrease in real incomes of the population, reduction in labour capacity, etc. There are several possible development scenarios for these processes. To eliminate their negative effects, it is necessary to determine which scenario takes place, since anti-crisis recommendations will vary for different scenarios.

It should be pointed out that in a real economy the agents do not always follow the optimal strategy. Moreover, external and other ill-predicted factors can affect demand. All of these result in the fact that the law of variation of v_t can differ from that considered above due to appearance of an additional component ξ^t, which in some cases could be considered as a random variable. In other words, instead of (8.3) the following equality holds

$$v_{t+1} = (1-\rho)v_t + \rho W^t + \xi^t, \qquad t = 0, 1, 2, \ldots, \tag{8.4}$$

where ξ^t is some sequence of random quantities. We will assume that for any t the quantity ξ^t is measurable relative to a σ-algebra, generated by $(v_0,\ldots,v_t)$, and bounded with probability one. Due to the obvious non-negativeness of v_t, it is reasonable to assume that ξ^t satisfies the condition

$$\xi^t \geq (\rho - 1)v_t - \rho W^t$$

with probability one.

Let us now analyze how the random actions ξ^t will affect the convergence of the sequence $\{v_t\}$ to the set of points $\{v^{(1)}, v^{(2)}\}$, defined above. Here, we will assume that the random actions are not too large on average as compared to the determinate trend $\rho(W^t - v_t)$. Let us denote the conditional mathematical expectation as $M(\bullet / \bullet)$. The following statement is true:

Theorem 2

Let $M(\xi^t / v_0, \ldots, v_t) = 0$, $M((\xi^t)^2 / v_0, \ldots, v_t) \leq \rho^2(W^t - v_t)^2$ be satisfied for any t with probability one. Let also $\rho<(2L)^{-1}$. Then, for the sequence $\{v_t, W^t\}$ defined according to (8.2) and (8.4) and for any $\varepsilon > 0$

$$P\{(W^t - v_t)^2 > \varepsilon\} \to 0$$

is satisfied as $t \to \infty$.

This theorem was also proved in Koshlai, Mikhalevich and Sergienko (1999).

8.4 The case with variable prices

In the previous section macroeconomic dynamics was analysed under two essential assumptions that, to the full extent, are not satisfied in the actual economy: the constancy of prices and the monopoly of the manufacturer-employer on the market of goods and services. This section develops the analysis without such assumptions.

The time t moves on continuously in the model considered below. By the analogy with the previous section we assume that the demand v at each succeeding moment $t+\Delta t$ will be the linear combination of demand at a moment of time t, its value is changed as price changes, and the real value of payment for the labour W at the same moment of time. If we denote such changed value of demand as $\bar{v}$, we obtain the following equation:

$$v(t+\Delta t) = ((1-\rho)\bar{v}(t) + \rho W(t))\Delta t, \tag{8.5}$$

where the coefficient $0<\rho<1$ does not depend on time and is sufficiently small. From the economic viewpoint, the first addend in (8.5) reflects the influence of previous savings and incomes that depend on the current sales volume, and the second addend reflects the effect of the current employees' incomes. Taking into account the aforesaid, we can assume that the value of $\bar{v}(t)$ consists of the following two parts and that one of them is inversely proportional to current prices $p(t)$, and that the other one does not depend on these prices:

$$\bar{v}(t) = \frac{v(t)}{p(t)}a + (1-a)v(t), \quad 0<a<1. \tag{8.6}$$

Here, the first addend reflects savings in native currency and also the fixed incomes of non-employees (for example, retirees and social security beneficiaries). The second addend reflects income obtained from commercial activity and foreign currency reserves.

Substituting (8.6) in (8.5) and passing to the limit as $\Delta t \to 0$, we obtain the differential equation

$$\dot{v} = \left((1-\rho)a\left(\frac{1}{p}-1\right)-\rho\right)v + \rho W, \tag{8.7}$$

due to the present author, where $W(t)$ is determined by (8.2) for the given time moment t.

Note that the last equation for $p = 1$ takes the form $dv/dt = -\rho v + \rho W$, which corresponds to (8.3) in the finite-difference case (assuming $dt = 1$).

In the considered model, the dynamics of prices is described by the Samuelson equation $\dot{p} = \lambda(\overline{D}(p) - \overline{S}(p))$, where $\overline{D}(p)$ is the current demand, $\overline{S}(p)$ is the commodity market supply, and $\lambda > 0$ is some coefficient. We assume that, in addition to the supply created by the monopolist-employer, there exists an alternative supply created by other manufacturers in the commodity market and also by the import of commodities (Dolan, Lindsey, 1994). Let the alternative supply function $\psi \in C^k$, $k \geq 4$, be a non-decreasing, upper-bounded, and concave one, i.e., it has all the properties of the competitive market supply function. Thus, in the model considered, the commodity market consists of two parts - namely, the competitive and the monopolistic ones. If the monopolistic component of supply exceeds the competitive one, then it is this component which determines the aggregate supply $\overline{S}(p) = \max(\psi(p), lS(W))$. From this, we obtain

$$\dot{p} = \lambda(v - \max(\psi(p), lS(W))). \tag{8.8}$$

Equations (8.2), (8.7), and (8.8) form the macroeconomic model here considered. Note that, in an actual economy, prices cannot be equal to zero and unlimited, and the demand rate is always non-negative and bounded. Therefore, the following conditions must be added to the equations specified:

$$p^* \leq p \leq p^{**};\ 0 \leq v \leq v^*, \tag{8.9}$$

that must be fulfilled for any moment of time $t \geq 0$. In what follows, we will assume that the minimum allowable price level p^* (corresponding to the prices of abandonment of production in the AS/AD model, Dolan, Lindsey, 1994), the maximum allowable price level p^{**}, and the maximum allowable demand rate v^* are time-independent. We consider the same mechanism of wage formation as in the previous section. Under the assumptions made, we will study the dynamics of solutions *p*(*t*) and *v*(*t*) of the equations obtained.

Let us denote

$$W = F(v) = \min\left(S^{-1}(\alpha l^{-1} v), (S')^{-1}\left(\frac{H}{l}\right)\right)$$

and assume that function *S* (*W*) is concave and differentiable in the set specified by inequalities (8.9).

From (8.7) and (8.8), we obtain the following system of differential equations and will consider it in the domain specified by inequalities (8.9):

$$\dot{v} = \left((1-\rho)a\left(\frac{1}{p}-1\right) - \rho \right)v + \rho F(v),$$

$$\dot{p} = \lambda\left(v - \max(\psi(p), lS(F(v)))\right). \tag{8.10}$$

The system (8.10) is a non-standard mathematical model since its right-hand side contains the operations of search for the maximum and the minimum. To analyse the dynamics of the system (8.10), we will construct a vector field, namely, the field of rates of changes in $(p(t), v(t))$. To this end, we find the curves on the plane (p, v) that satisfy inequalities (8.9) and on which the right-hand side of the first or second equation of the system (8.10) becomes zero. The points at which the right hand sides of both equations of this system become zeros are the states of the system's (8.10) equilibrium. The mentioned curves and the equilibrium states play a key role in studying the dynamics of the system (8.10) in the phase space formed by all the initial conditions satisfying inequalities (8.9).

We denote

$$c = (S')^{-1}\left(\frac{H}{l}\right), \tilde{v} = lS(c), \quad g(p) = (1-\rho)a\left(\frac{1}{p}-1\right) - \rho .$$

The function $g(p)$ has the unique zero at the point $\bar{p}$, $0 < \bar{p} < 1$. If $p > \bar{p}$, then the function $g(p) < 0$ and monotonically decreases.

In investigating the dynamics of system (8.10), we will distinguish between the cases where ρ is small and where ρ is not small.

We start from the second case. We assume that $p^* > \bar{p}$.

Let us consider the curve $\hat{L}$ that is specified by the conditions $g(p)v + p\tilde{v} = 0, p > p^*$, and $\tilde{v} \le v \le v^*$.

It is obvious that $\hat{L}$ is the plot of a monotonously decreasing differentiable function defined on an interval $[p^*, \tilde{p}]$. In this case, we assume that $\tilde{p} > 1$. Let us consider the function S. It is obvious that its inverse function S^{-1} is convex, differentiable, and unbounded above. The solutions of the system (8.10) are further analyzed under the assumptions given below.

1. The set of solutions of the equation

$$g(p)v + \rho S^{-1}(\alpha l^{-1} v) = 0 \tag{8.11}$$

is not empty. Then, as it is easy to see, there exists $p_m > 0$ such that, for each $p > p_m$, the equation (8.11) has two roots $0 < V_1(p) < V_2(p)$, and, at the same time, $V_1(p)$ is a monotonously decreasing and $V_2(p)$ is a monotonously increasing function of p. The functions $V_1(p)$ and $V_2(p)$ belong to the space $C^k, k \geq 4$. These functions assume identical values at the point p_m.

2. The inequality $p_m < \widetilde{p}$ is true.
3. The inequality $V_1(p_m) < \widetilde{v}$ is true.
4. The function $\psi(p)$ is bounded and there exists a point $p_b > \widetilde{p}$ such that the conditions $\psi(p) < \widetilde{v}$ and $\psi(p_b) = \widetilde{v}$ are true for all $p^* \leq p < p_b$.
5. The equation

$$\psi(p) = v^* \tag{8.12}$$

has a solution p_b^* and, at the same time, there is $p_b^* < p^{**}$.

6. The set $L_S = \{ (p, V_1(p)) : p \geq p_m, V_1(p) \geq \psi(p)\}$ is not empty.

Conditions 1-5 provide for the dissipativity of the system (8.10) on the rectangle (8.9). Hence, the solutions of the system (8.10) with the initial conditions from (8.9) are extendable to the positive semi-axis and are within the rectangle (8.9).

We denote

$$L_U = \{(p, V_2(p)) : p \geq p_m, V_2(p) \leq \widetilde{v}\},\ \Psi = \{(p, \psi(p)), p > p^*\}.$$

By virtue of conditions 1-5, the curves $\hat{L}$ and L_U have a common point $(\widetilde{p}, \widetilde{v})$. Since the function V_1 monotonously decreases, the function $\psi(p)$ monotonously decreases, and the set L_s is not empty, the equation $V_1(p) = \psi(p)$ has a unique solution $p_{\max} > p_m$.

We now turn back to the above-mentioned analogy with the model with three equilibrium points, which is considered in section 8.3. Two of them (the upper one $v^{(2)}$ when the quantity W depends on H, and the lower one $\overline{v}^{(1)}$ when this quantity is determined by the demand v with stable prices) are the points of stable equilibrium, and the intermediate point $\hat{v}^{(1)}$ is unstable. The points of the curve $\hat{L}$ are the analogues of the upper equilibrium point, the points from L_U are the analogues of the intermediate point, and the points from L_S are the analogues of the lower point.

Lines L_U and L_S separate the area of demand growth (outside these lines) from the area of demand decline (between the lines) in the case when wage foundation is determined by employer on the basis of demand for produced goods. Line $\hat{L}$ separates the mentioned areas for the case when employer determines wage foundation based on marginal utility of labour and marginal labour cost.

The curves L_U, L_S, $\hat{L}$ and Ψ subdivide the phase space of the system (8.10) into domains with different behaviours of the vector field. We denote these domains by D^{z_1, z_2}, where z_1 is the sign of the right-hand side of the price equation or 0, and z_2 is the sign of the right-hand side of the demand equation or 0. The structure of the vector field is presented in Figure A8.4a. We describe the domains obtained.

The set D^{++} is bounded by the segments $\{(p^*, v), \widetilde{v} \le v \le v^*\}$, $\{(p, \widetilde{v}), p^* \le p \le \widetilde{p}\}$, and the curve $\hat{L}$. The boundary of the domain D^{+-} is formed by the curve $\hat{L}$, an arc of the curve $\psi(p)$, and the segment $\{(p, \widetilde{v}), \widetilde{p} \le p \le p_b^*\}$. The domain D^{0-} is bounded by the curve L_S, an arc of the curve L_U, an arc of the curve Ψ, and the segment $\{(p, \widetilde{v}), \widetilde{p} \le p \le p_b^*\}$. The domain D^{--} is adjacent to D^{0-} and D^{+-}, and to the boundary D^{--} belongs an arc of the curve $\psi(p)$ and the plot of the function V_1 (p). The curvilinear sector D^{-+} is bounded by a part of the plot of the function V_1 (p) and an arc of the curve $\psi(p)$. The domain D^{0+} is a set whose boundary contains an arc of the curve $\psi(p)$, an arc of the curve L_U, the curve L_S, and the segment $\{(p, \widetilde{v}), p^* \le p \le \widetilde{p}\}$.

We denote by L the set of all the stationary points of the system (8.10). It is obvious that we have $L = L_S \cup L_U$ and that, for the points of the curve $\hat{L}$, the right hand side of the price dynamics equation remains positive. Let $V_1(p_m) = V_{\text{m}}$. The set L_S considered without the point (p_m, V_m), is the set of all stable equilibrium states of the system (8.10). The set L_U consists of unstable equilibrium states of the system (8.10).

We denote by $p(t) = p(t, p, v)$, $v(t) = v(t, p, v)$ the solution of the system (8.10); this solution satisfies the conditions $p(0) = p$ and $v(0)=v$, where the point (p, v) satisfies conditions (8.9).

Definition 1

We call the system (10) stabilizable if, for any point (p, v) of the phase space of the system (10), there exists a point (p_+, v_+) such that we have

$$\lim_{t \to \infty}(p(t, p, v), v(t, p, v)) = (p_+, v_+). \tag{8.13}$$

Definition 2

We call the stabilization set of the system (8.10) the set of all the points (p_+, v_+) *for which equation (8.13) is true.*

Note that we can consider the concept of a stabilizable system as an analogy of the convergence concept for a system with discrete time used in section 8.3, and the concept of a stabilization set as an analogy of the limiting points set concept.

Let us find the stabilization conditions of the system (8.10). We assume that $\widetilde{p} > p_{\max}$. Semantically, this assumption means that, for different prices, the commodity market supply can be determined by the amounts of products provided by both the monopolist-employer and the alternative competitive supply. This segment of the market cannot be considered as completely closed or as completely open to competition.

It is obvious that the system (8.10) belongs to the class of piecewise smooth systems. In what follows, we use the terminology from the theory of dynamic systems, which is commonly accepted in the classical (smooth) case (Andronov *et al.*, 1996; Arnold *et al.*, 1986; Kuznetsov, 1998; Chow, Mallet-Paret, 1977). We will not stipulate the choice of some term or another in view of the existing analogy. Let us consider a separatrix going out from the point (p_m, V_m). We denote a phase point moving along the separatrix by $(p^s(t), v^s(t))$. Let $(p^s(0), v^s(0)) \in D^{0+}$. Then we have $p^s(t) = p^s(0)$, and $v^s(t)$ monotonously increases. From the economic viewpoint, this means that the prices remain unchangeable with increasing demand; hence, the expansion in production volume is proportional to demand. We note that such processes are inherent in the growth stage of the classical business cycle. After intersecting the right line $v = \widetilde{v}$, the payment for labour ceases to change proportionally to demand, an imbalance between supply and demand takes place, and this imbalance results in inflation. In the domain D^{++}, the functions $p^s(t)$ and $v^s(t)$ are monotonously increasing. A growth accompanied by inflation is inherent in the boom stage of the classical business cycle. A rise in prices decelerates demand. After transverse intersection of the curve $\hat{L}$, the phase point passes to the domain D^{+-}, where $p^s(t)$ monotonously increases and $v^s(t)$ monotonously decreases. By this time, the boom is replaced by a decline, which is aggravated by a depreciation of savings through inflation. If the phase point intersects the right line $v = \widetilde{v}$, then the payment for labour is beginning to change again proportionally to the demand. As a consequence, the feedback "a decrease in demand - a decrease in payment for labour - a decrease in demand" arises and accelerates the decline. In the domain D^{0-}, the function $p^s(t)$ remains constant, $v^s(t)$ monotonously decreases, and the decline assumes the features of overproduction crisis. In the domain D^{--}, to which the phase point passes after intersecting the line $\psi(\bullet)$, the oversupply is beginning to impact on the prices, and $p^s(t)$ and $v^s(t)$ will be monotonously decreasing functions. The incipient deflation (a decrease in prices) decelerates the decline and increases the value of retained assets. The combination of deflation and overcooling is typical of the depression stage of the classical business cycle. After intersecting the plot of the function $V_1(p)$, the phase point passes to the domain D^{-+}, where $p^s(t)$ monotonously decreases and $v^s(t)$ increases. The processes that run in this domain are typical of the initial stages of the revival phase of the business cycle. Thus, the order of transition of the specified phase space domains by the phase point corresponds with the order of all the basic stages of business activity.

At some moment $t = T^s$, the phase point $(p^s(t), v^s(t))$ intersects the curve Ψ. It follows from the condition $\widetilde{p} > p_{\max}$ that we have $p^s(T^s) < p_{\max}$. The following two cases are possible: $p^s(T^s) \leq p_m$ and $p^s(T^s) > p_m$. We first consider the second case. In the domain D^{0+}, we have $p^s(t) = p^s(T^s) = \hat{p}$ and $v^s(t) \to V_1(\hat{p}) = \hat{V}$ as $t \to \infty$. Then the separatrix enters a point $(\hat{p}, \hat{V}) \in L_S$. This case is presented in Figure A8.4a. We denote $\lambda = \hat{p} - p_m$. It is obvious that, in this case, we have $\lambda > 0$. In the first case, the system is not stabilizable when $\lambda = p^s(T^s) - p_m < 0$. This case is presented in Figure A8.4b. We note that, for the particular case where $\lambda = 0$, the system (8.10) is also unstabilizable and the separatrix outgoing from the point (p_m, V_m) enters the system. Hereafter, we will call such a curve homoclinic. It is presented in Figure A8.4c. The basic business cycle in its "pure" form (without a long-term economic growth) corresponds to the movement of the point along this curve.

It is obvious that the quantity λ does not depend upon the choice of the initial point on the separatrix. We assume that we have $\widetilde{p} > p_{\max}$. Then the case is possible where $(p^s(t), v^s(t))$ intersects the right line $v = \widetilde{v}$ at the point $(p^s(T^s), v^s(T^s))$ such that $p^s(T^s) < p_{\max}$. In this case, the separatrix also enters a point $(\hat{p}, \hat{V}) \in L_S$ and we have $\lambda > 0$. From the above reasoning, we obtain the statements formulated and proved in Belan, Mikhalevich and Sergienko (2003).

Theorem 3

Suppose the assumptions 1-5 are fulfilled. In order for the system (8.10) to be stabilizable, it is necessary that the separatrix outgoing from the point (p_m, V_m) *enter a point that belongs to* L_S *and does not coincide with the point* (p_m, V_m).

Let us find the stability criterion of the system (8.10). To this end, we consider an arbitrary point $(p, \psi(p))$ such that $p < p_m$. Denote by $p(t) = p(t, p)$, $v(t)=v(t,p)$ the solution of the system (8.10) that satisfies the condition $p(0) = p,\ v(0) = \psi(p)$.

By analogy with the above reasoning, we arrive at the conclusion that there exists the least positive T^1 such that the point $(p(t), v(t))$ intersects the curve Ψ. We denote $p(T^1) = P(p)$.

Definition 3

We call a function $p \to P(p)$ *defined on the interval* $[p^*, p_m)$ *the successor function of system (8.10).*

Under the above conditions, the successor function exists and is differentiable over the interval $[p^*, p_m)$. It follows from the definition of the successor function that the statement given below is true.

Theorem 4

Suppose the conditions of Theorem 3 are fulfilled. In order for the system (8.10) to be stabilizable, it is necessary and sufficient that $P(p) > p$ *and system (8.10) have no homoclinic curve.*

Conditions of the cycle appearance were formulated and analyzed on the basis of the latter statement.

The analysis shows that the determining factor influencing the dynamics of the system (8.10) is the relative position of the curves L_S and Ψ. For a low (relative to L_S) position of Ψ, the system is stabilizable and its set of stabilization consists of equilibrium points analogous to those for systems considered in section 8.3. A change in prices will not exert an appreciable effect on the conclusions. For a high position of Ψ, the situation changes. System (8.10) has solutions that orbitally converge to stable periodic solutions whose characteristics correspond to the basic business cycle. Depending on the initial state of the system, the convergence will be accompanied by the general tendency towards an economic growth or a decline. In this case, the rates of growth (or decline) will decrease and approach the periodic regime.

In the case where the set L_S degenerates into the point $(\overline{p},\overline{v})$, the trajectories of the system that originate not far from $(\overline{p},\overline{v})$ are unfolding or folding spirals. For an economy with the monopsonic labour market and a completely competitive market of goods and services, business cycles are repeated with increasing or decreasing amplitudes and with different duration. For more detailed consideration of this case see Belan, Mikhalevich and Sergienko (2003).

8.5 Conclusions

1. According to the model considered, a macroeconomic system with a monopsonic labour market and predominantly monopolized commodity market of goods and services passes to an equilibrium state after some transitional process.

Depending on the initial conditions, such a state could be a point of the curve L_S. The lower equilibrium point in the model with stable prices corresponds to this point in which the rate of manufacture's monopoly profit is maximum. The points of the curve L_U, as well as an intermediate equilibrium point of the model from section 8.3, are the points of unstable equilibrium. In contrast to the model mentioned, the model with variable prices has no upper equilibrium state since the approach of the system towards it will be accompanied by the excess of demand over supply with a constant level of total wage fund. It leads to inflation, depreciates previous savings, lowers demand, and directs the economy to the lower equilibrium point. Thus, if an economy is highly monopolized and external shocks and exogenous technological changes affecting the values of its parameters are absent, then, after some period, the economic growth ends. The development comes to the end when prices and volume of products are such that they provide the greatest superprofit to monopolists.

2. In contrast to a monopolized economy, the cycling of the periods of growth and recession is characteristic of an economy with a monopsonic labour market and a partially competitive (mixed) market of goods and services. Such dynamics corresponds to the basic business cycle observable in the nineteenth century and in the early twentieth century. According to the results of modeling, the determining role in passing from growth to recession is played by the consumer savings inflationary depreciation, and such a role in passing from recession (depression) to growth is played by a deflationary increase in the value of assets. The major cause of cyclicity is the interaction of competitive market of goods and services capable (from the viewpoint of the majority of economic theorists) of providing self-regulation under the conditions of economic

growth, and the monopsonic labour market that is not a self-controllable one and allows for only a limited growth level (up to a definite level of production). In the case where the curve Ψ passes through the point $(\bar{p},\bar{v})$, i.e., when the market of goods and services is competitive with any price level, the cyclic character of development becomes slack and the economy passes to simple reproduction or becomes stronger. The crisis character of changing the system's behaviour when its parameters pass through critical values should be particularly noted.

3. The monopsony in a labour market provides employers with the greatest income over a bounded time interval. However, an economy with such a labour market with different (monopoly, mixed, or competitive) forms of organization of the market of goods and services demonstrates its incapacity for development and stable growth. In this case (in the long run) the entire society, including employers, suffers losses. Since statistical data (Mikhalevich, Koshlai and Khmil, 1998) indicate that monopsonic relations are prevalent in some countries with a transition economy, the creation of a competitive labour market should be an important task of structural economic reforms. This problem can be tackled in the following ways.

The first is the development of small and medium-sized businesses, which will absorb the most qualified labour and will create the non-monopolized component of the labour market demand.

The second is support for trade union movements, which can restrict the employers' power at the labour market and will transform the latter into the market with two-side competition.

No doubt, a reasonable labour policy at the early stages of transition is based on the combination of these two ways.

The consequences of imperfect competition at the labour market require further research, including that with the use of mathematical modeling. Such research could be realized, in particular, along the following directions:

(1) analysis of the effect of the labour market with bilateral monopoly competition (monopolists-employers against trade unions) on the economic dynamics at whole;
(2) estimation of the effect of external demand shocks (for example, random changes in export turnover) and subjective employer's expectations of change in labour payment under the conditions of monopsony;
(3) analysis of models with supply functions that differ from the considered ones and reflect the interaction between the monopolized and competitive segments of the commodity market;

(4) investigations into an economy with a partially (for some branch segments) monopolized labour market;
(5) further theoretical economic interpretation of the results achieved.

References

Andronov, A., Leontovich, Ye.A., Gordon, I.I., Mayer, A.G. (1996) *Qualitative Theory of Dynamic Systems of the Second Order* [in Russian]. Moscow: Nauka.

Arnold, V.I., V.S. Afraimovich, Yu.S. Il'yashenko, L.P. Shil'nikov (1986) Bifurcation Theory. *Modern Problems of Mathematics.* Moscow: VINITI, vol. 5, pp 5-218.

Aslund, A. and R. Layard (1993) *Changing the Economic System in Russia.* London: Printer Publishing.

Belan, Ye.P., M.V. Mikhalevich, and I.V. Sergienko (2003) Cyclic Economic Processes in Systems with Monopsonic Labour Markets. *Cybernetics and Systems Analysis*, **39**(4), 488-500.

Boal, W. (1995) Testing for Employer Monopsony in Turn-of-the-Century Coal Mining. *RAND Journal of Economics*, **26**, 519-36.

Bortis, H. (1997) *Institutions, Behaviour and Economic Theory.* Cambridge: University Press.

Chow S. and J. Mallet-Paret (1977) Integral Averaging and Bifurcation. *Journal of Differential Equations*, **26**, 112-59.

Ciupagea, C. and G. Turlea (1997) A Study upon the Labour Market in the Industry Sector of the Romanian Economy. *ACE Project P 95-2001.* Bucharest: University of Bucharest.

Commander, S. and F. Coricelli (1995) Unemployment, Restructuring and the Labour Market in Eastern Europe and Russia. Washington DC: The World Bank.

Dolan, E.G. and D.E. Lindsey (1994) *Macroeconomics* (Russian translation). Saint Petersburg: Litera Plus.

Koshlai, L.B., M.V. Mikhalevich and I.V. Sergienko (1999) Simulation of Employment and Growth Processes in a Transition Economy. *Cybernetics and Systems Analysis*, **35**(3), 392-405.

Kuznetzov, Y.A. (1998) *Elements of Applied Bifurcation Theory.* New York: Springer-Verlag.

Manning, A. (2003) *Monopsony in Motion: Imperfect Competition in Labour Markets.* Princeton, NJ: Princeton University Press.

Mikhalevich, M., L. Koshlai and R. Khmil (1998) Multisectoral Models of labour Supply for Countries in Transition. *Research Memorandum, ACE Project No. 98/9*, University of Leicester, Leicester.

Polterovich, V.H. (2003) Paradoxes of the Russian Labour Market and the Theory of Collective Frms. *Economics and Mathematical Methods*, **39**(2), 210-17.

Robinson, J. (1933) *Economics of Imperfect Competition.* Cambridge: Cambridge University Press.

Robinson, J. (1962) *Essays in the Theory of Economic Growth.* London: Macmillan.

Appendix

Table A8.1 Rates of GDP growth/decline in transition countries during the deepest recession (%)

Country \ Year	1991	1992	1993	1994	1995	1996
Bulgaria	-11.7	-7.3	-2.4	1.8	2.6	-10.3
Czech Republic	-14.2	-6.4	-0.9	2.6	4.8	4.5
Hungary	-11.9	-3.1	-0.6	2.9	1.5	0.5
Kazakhstan	-13.0	-14.0	-12.0	-25.0	-8.9	1.4
Latvia	-10.4	-34.9	-14.0	0.6	-0.8	2.8
Lithuania	-13.4	0.37	-24.2	1.0	3.0	3.6
Poland	-7.0	2.6	3.8	5.2	7.0	6.0
Romania	-12.9	-8.8	1.3	3.9	6.9	4.3
Russia	-13.0	-14.5	-8.7	-12.6	-4.0	-6.3
Slovak Republic	-14.6	-6.5	-3.7	4.9	6.8	6.9
Ukraine	-9.0	-10.0	-14.0	-23.0	-11.8	-11.9

Source: Statistical tables. *Economics of Transition* (1997), **5**(1), 255-70; and **5**(2), 521-52.

Table A8.2 Unemployment in transition countries during the deepest recession (% of the labour force, end-year)

Country \ Year	1991	1992	1993	1994	1995	1996
Bulgaria	11.5	15.6	16.4	12.8	10.5	12.5
Czech Republic	4.1	2.6	3.5	3.2	2.9	3.5
Hungary	7.5	12.3	12.1	10.4	10.4	10.5
Kazakhstan	0	0.5	0.6	1.6	2.4	3.5
Latvia	n/a	2.3	5.8	6.5	6.6	7.2
Lithuania	0.3	1.3	4.4	3.8	6.2	7.0
Poland	11.8	13.6	16.4	16.0	14.9	13.6
Romania	n/a	6.2	9.2	11.0	9.9	7.8
Russia	n/a	n/a	5.5	7.1	8.2	9.3
Slovak Republic	11.8	10.3	14.4	14.8	13.1	12.8
Ukraine*	0	0.3	0.4	0.4	0.6	1.2

*Official data. Unofficial estimates of unemployment do not exceed 8-10 per cent.
Source: Statistical tables. *Economics of Transition* (1997), **5**(1), 255-270; and **5**(2), 521-52.

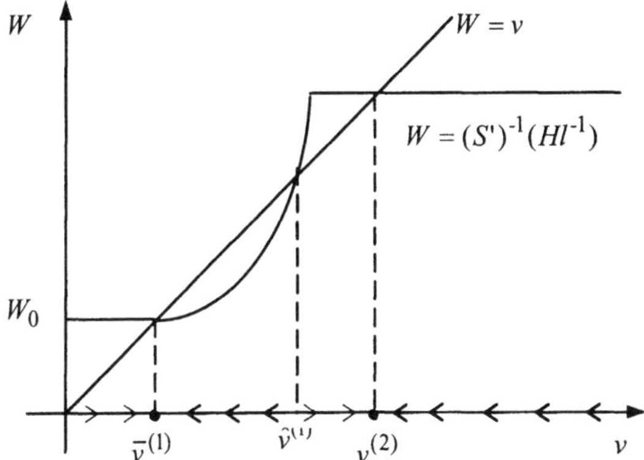

Figure A8.1 Three equilibrium points

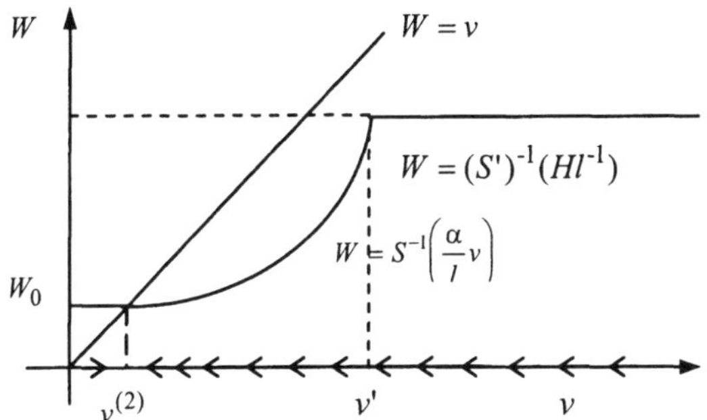

Figure A8.2 One equilibrium point

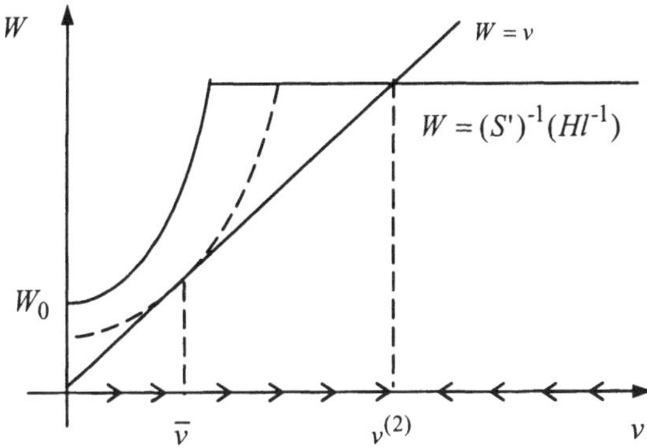

Figure A8.3 Two equilibrium points

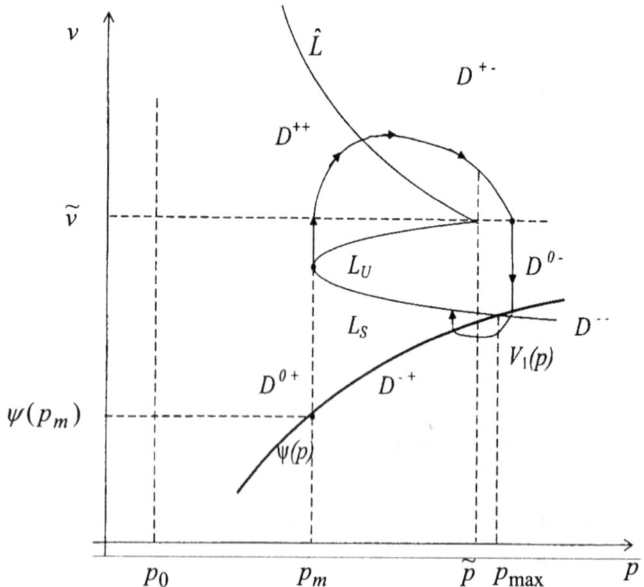

Figure A8.4a Phase space. Stabilization for λ > 0
—►► - separatrix

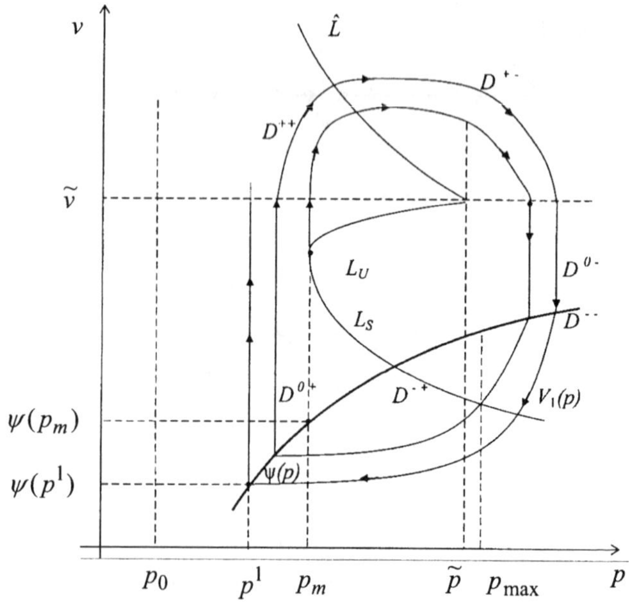

Figure A8.4b Cycles for λ < 0
—►► - separatrix

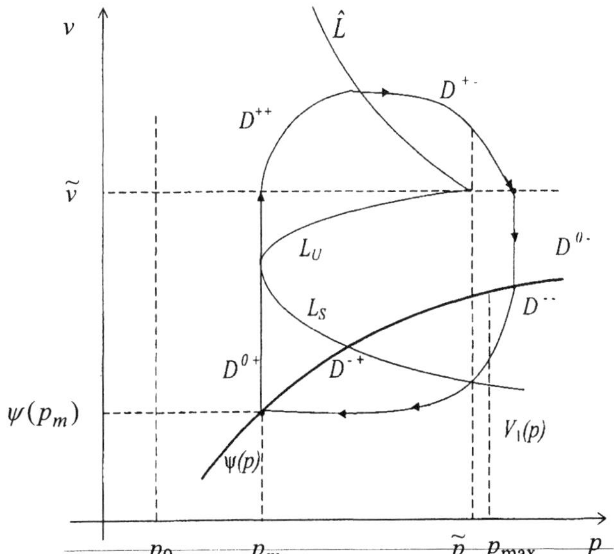

Figure A8.4c Homoclinic curve for $\lambda = 0$

—►►- homoclinic curve

Index